"This book is loaded with great ideas to help you to be more successful in every area of your life."
  – Brian Tracy, Author, *Change Your Thinking, Change Your Life*

"This book gives you the formula for success. Read it, study it, and then go to work!"
  – Steve Siebold, author, *How Rich People Think*

"*The Power to have it All* book is a practical and inspirational set of strategies designed to create a meaningful and successful life. The tone is warm, upbeat and understanding while the step-by-step approach to creating massive success is down to earth. The stories in this book will inspire you to be more, do more, and give more. This book is a must read for all those hungry for massive success."
  – Nick Nanton, 5-Time Emmy Award Winning Director

"*The Power to have it All* is an excellent resource for people seeking tools to lead them to success. It is written in a conversational style which keeps it simple. The tools in the book are laid out in a logical manner so they are easy to apply. Take the journey and you will have the foundation to achieve massive success."
  – Mike Allan, Manager, Completions & Well Servicing,
    Cenovus Energy

"Inspiring and engaging story of Dr Ayee's journey. Through many clear and concise examples he shows the power of habits to create massive and enduring success in your life."
  – Alex Cardenas, Director, Strategy, Business Development &
    Optimization, Husky Energy

"*The Power to have it All* enables the reader to reflect on what is possible with the gift of an inner strength to believe in oneself and overcome the existing systems, barriers and surrounding noise that continually challenge our own strengths and dreams. George Ayee successfully challenges the reader to step forward and energize oneself to go beyond our own limits and society's constraints to become a massive success!"
  – Andrew Mardon, SCM Manager, Procurement Service Center,
    Husky Energy

The
POWER
to have it
ALL

The DNA for MASSIVE SUCCESS

Proven Strategies for Maximum Results

Dr. George Ayee

Published by
Hasmark Publishing, judy@hasmarkservices.com

Disclaimer

This book is designed to provide information and motivation to our readers. It is sold with the understanding that the publisher is not engaged to render any type of psychological, legal, or any other kind of professional advice. The content of each article is the sole expression and opinion of its author, and not necessarily that of the publisher. No warranties or guarantees are expressed or implied by the publisher's choice to include any of the content in this volume. Neither the publisher nor the individual author(s) shall be liable for any physical, psychological, emotional, financial, or commercial damages, including, but not limited to, special, incidental, consequential or other damages. Our views and rights are the same: You are responsible for your own choices, actions, and results.

Permission should be addressed in writing to georgeayee@shaw.ca

Editor, Nita Robinson, Nita Helping Hand? www.NitaHelpingHand.com

Cover Design and Layout, Anne Karklins
annekarklins@gmail.com

ISBN-13: 978-1-988071-36-7
ISBN-10: 1988071364

Hasmark
PUBLISHING

*I dedicate this book to
my mum, Lydia N. A. Ayee, who inspired me to be more, do more
and give more; Dr. I. S. Kiggundu who saw greatness in me
and gave me the opportunity to exploit my potential to the full;
my special relatives who have been part of my life journey
and success; my siblings; my great friends who have been with me
through the highs and lows; those hungry for massive success;
and writers, speakers, coaches who inspired me through their books,
conferences, and seminars. Thanks a million!*

Contents

Introduction

Millions around the world are looking for the code to success, achievement, and advancement. You are looking for the code to massive success and advancement. The formula or key to achieving massive success is progressive, consistent and relentless effort in taking massive action in alignment with what you want to achieve. It's also about creating your own opportunities, removing roadblocks, sidestepping challenges, leaving your customers and everyone you meet with an impression of increase, using your knowledge and skills to bring significant value to the marketplace and a focus on exponential growth as opposed to traditional growth. Whatever you need or require in achieving massive success is already built into you. You are engineered for massive success and you are capable of exponential growth and improvement through quantum leaps. You can achieve massive results beyond your imagination when you break out of the mold you are encased in. The mold of self-imposed limitations, negative talk, broken focus, wrong thinking, wrong associations, indecision, limited action and the limitations others have placed on you. If you were like me, I was brought up to think that success can only be attained through gradual, incremental and massive effort. Massive effort without proper direction is wasted time and wasted life. Massive effort can just be motion, but what you really need is massive action in the right direction and on the right things. You might say that massive success is too far out; I recommend you just do the ordinary things in an extraordinary way and you will get the results you are aiming for. Don't be intimidated by the word massive, just crank up the great things you are already doing a notch and you will be on your way to taking massive action on a consistent basis.

How do you release the talent, passion, genius and gifts you already have inside you for massive success? It all begins with the awareness that what you need to achieve massive success is already wired into you when you came into this world. Circumstances and life challenges may put a lid on your gifting. Take off the lid of your limitations and allow the real you to break out. Keep up the momentum when you start taking massive action in tandem with the future you want to create. There should be no relenting once you get started. Momentum is the name of the game. Let no one kid you with make-believe, simple formulas for success. You are more intelligent than that. To achieve massive success, you have to do the work, make mistakes, learn from your mistakes, and keep going until – and I mean until – you find 'gold'. The journey to achieving massive success is dotted with adversity, challenges, and obstacles; what you need is continuous focus, mental toughness and inspiring yourself to the finish line.

You need continuous focus and mental toughness to achieve massive success!

Some folks have invested heavily in personal development resources, have attended several achievement motivation programs, success workshops and seminars, and yet continue to feel stuck. Do you feel like you have hit the wall and are looking for ways around it? Do you have talents that you are not leveraging or a passion to change people's lives and yet you find yourself going around in circles? There is a way to achieve massive success and you can when you work for it. Why would I say something like that? Because I know without any reservation whatsoever that you were born for more, born for a life of increase, born to leave everyone you meet with an impression of increase. I also know that we live in an abundant and opulent universe. The key to tapping into this abundance and opulence is to operate from a creative plane rather than a competitive plane. Think your way into the results and the future you want to create.

I know a gentleman called Mark (not his real name to disguise his identity), who invested thousands of dollars in various books, attended seminars from "who is who" in personal development, but still did not have much to show for it. Mark is frustrated and thinking that success and achievement is an elusive thing. Here is the truth; if knowledge and more knowledge was the key to success, Mark and all the others would be living their dreams by now. You may be stuck wondering why success and achievement is so elusive, just like Mark had concluded. You may be feeling frustrated and disillusioned. You are not alone. There are millions around the globe who are searching fervently to crack the code to success. These people, including you, are looking for the combination numbers to success and achievement. Knowing is not the same as doing. There is a gap between knowing and doing and you have to close that gap to be successful in whatever you want to do and achieve. In my seminars, I speak to individuals and leaders about change and transformation and it's only those who translate the knowledge into action that succeed in the end. There is also a gap between what you believe to be true and what you actually do to reflect what you belief. Success is a precise science in that if you replicate what successful people do, you will be able to achieve success as well. Successful people do things a certain way while unsuccessful people do things a different way. Your current results come from your beliefs, thoughts, feelings, actions and all that you do on a daily basis. You can never be any different from what you habitually do on a day-to-day basis. There is a way to achieve massive success, fulfil your potential, and achieve your heart desires and wants – not just your needs – and this is hidden in your daily routine.

Your Success is hidden in what you do daily!

I wrote this book for you and the millions around the globe who feel stuck, those who are not exploiting their potential to the maximum, those who want to leverage their passion for profit, and those thinking that success and achievement is only for a special few; all those who have invested thousands of dollars in personal development programs and resources without much to show for it. Is success that difficult? Yes it is! Success takes time, energy and effort; you need to know the combination numbers to open the doors of success. If you are willing to do what successful people do and invest the time to take the necessary actions, you will achieve your goals. I have been a student of success and achievement for years and continue to be a student because I am a life-long learner. The day I stop learning and investing in myself will be the day I begin the journey of regression. Success means different things to different people. I like the definition by Earl Nightingale who defined success as "The progressive realization of a worthy ideal". This definition says you are a success for as long as you are progressively moving in the direction of your dreams and fulfilling your potential. To the teacher in the classroom, success is inspiring young minds to fulfil their potential; to the entrepreneur, making profits and growing the business; to the mother, to bring up the children in the best way possible. To me, success means releasing champions and inspiring each person to greatness. When you succeed, I succeed. I am addicted to seeing people succeed massively and I want to leave every single person I meet with an impression of increase, for each one needs all of us! What is your definition of success? What does winning in life mean to you? What is your definition of massive success? You are engineered for success and you have the seeds of greatness within you.

You have the seeds of greatness within you!

My Journey to Success

My story started with a quest for a great life, to fulfil my potential and achieve my dreams. I had this great desire to win in life and impact people's lives for good. I come from a family of seven. One great guy who led the way and three set of twins following. I am a middle twin. My parents gave me the name Gift, which I later unilaterally changed to George because some of the kids in the neighborhood and school were making fun of me, calling me 'parcel' which infuriated and embarrassed me at the same time. At the subconscious level, I had this premonition that my parents gave me that name for a reason so I started believing that my name 'Gift' meant be a gift to the people around me, the world, and do something with my life for the benefit of others. My parents ingrained in me at the time that knowledge through education was the best way to achieve my goals and be successful. This is what they were told by their parents I believe. With this belief and matching orders, I enrolled in a university outside my country. There was a catch though. My parents did not have the money to support my education so that meant looking for work to pay my way through school. The University was gracious and put me on a work-study program to help pay part of the fees. I visited different organizations to ask for financial support with no success. On one occasion, I visited an organization and was advised by the leader of the organization to just go back home and find something else to do. I talked to my parents about my challenges in getting financial support and the struggles I was going through. As you can expect from any loving parent, my dad suggested I return home to work for a printing and publishing business he was thinking about setting up. This business never got off the ground. I told my dad I was not returning home until I achieved my purpose for leaving home. I took whatever job was available at the university through work-study and completed my bachelor's degree.

After completing my bachelor's degree, I looked for a job but could not find any. The excuse from the potential employers at the time was that I did not have any work experience. In my naivety, I asked one of the employers, "If you don't give me a job, how do you expect me to get the work experience?" to which he said, "We are not a charitable organization; I don't care what you think. I have no job for you."I volunteered to work for a charitable organization and got my first work experience to put on my resume. I did more volunteering for other organizations and got even more experience.

Still, with no job in sight I applied for a Master of Business Administration degree in England. I was accepted and commenced the MBA program. I found a benevolent Catholic priest who promised to pay part of my fees in return for working with him in Africa. Once again I requested for work-study at the university to pay a portion of the fees and got office cleaning jobs to keep me afloat for a while. Whatever money I was making was inadequate to fully pay the rest of the fees so I was in arrears. The university administration gave me an ultimatum to pay up or they would let me go. I remember doing all that I knew to do, taking on more work and going to class half asleep because I had worked all night. I went to the MBA director's personal assistant with the suggestion to quit because the challenges were too much for me. Her words to me were so clear; "George, do not quit now. If you do, you will regret it for the rest of your life. You have come this far and I know you will finish. Don't give up on yourself now." I took her advice and continued with the courses, worked various jobs and completed the master's program. On graduation day, I was awarded the MBA Director's Award of Distinction with the following accompanying words from the professor: "George, use this degree and award to change and influence your part of the world." These words resonated with me and are now part of my personal vision statement which says, "I release champions and inspire each one to greatness." I have since obtained a doctorate degree in business administration, worked with international management consulting firms, started two private universities, worked with multinational corporations, set up a consulting practice providing training and consulting services to for-profit and non-profit organizations, set up a health and wellness business, and now engaged in professional speaking on change and transformation for optimal results and coaching services to clients in various countries. My story is not to impress you but rather to impress upon you that you can be successful in life and achieve the goals you have set for yourself. I want to inspire you and reignite the passion you once had. I want to rekindle your lost dreams and set you on a course to achieve massive success. In speaking to thousands and conducting seminars around the world, I came to one conclusion: You can change the trajectory of your life, you can move the needle positively in the direction of your dreams, you can achieve your ambition and leave the world a better place, and you have the internal resources to follow your passion and make money living your passion. You sure can profit from your passion!

Massive Action, Massive Results

To achieve massive success or results, you need massive action. Results are the name of the game, so ensure you keep this front and center in all you do. Without the results to show for your efforts and actions, you are just wasting your time and wasting your life. Life is not a dress rehearsal and everything you do on a daily basis is creating the life you want and the life you don't want. Every single day contributes to your future success! At the end of each chapter are **Action Exercises for Massive Success** to help you internalize the strategies, ideas and concepts and to cause you to take action, provoke you to question your current results, and take the necessary steps to move you toward what you want in life. It is very easy to get caught up in reading and skipping the action exercises because you want to finish the book and move on to the next. I have done this myself when I started the journey of success. I must confess that skipping the exercises like I did in the past did not serve me well at all. I completed reading lots of books but never cemented the strategies, principles, and ideas in my mind. Your results come from doing and taking action so I suggest you don't skip over the exercises. These exercises are for self-introspection, honing down the strategies and taking corrective actions in alignment with the results you want to get. Go make it Big Time and leave your mark! The world is waiting for you!

Every single day contributes to your future success!

Chapter One

Who Am I

You are pure potential!

> *"The will to win, the desire to succeed, the urge to*
> *reach your full potential... these are the keys that will*
> *unlock the door to personal excellence."*
> ~ *Confucius*

You can experience an exceptional quality of life filled with joy, excitement, happiness, love, creativity and fulfillment when you strive to reach your full potential. Reaching your full potential is the highest expression of your life. Every human being was born for a life of increase. We are always looking for avenues for increase. We want more joy, happiness, promotion, education, connection with God, great relationships, love, money, career advancement, financial freedom, and so on. Your potential is unlimited and if you know the full extent of all that you can accomplish, it will amaze you. The question is, why not? You can unlock your full potential by intentionally making a conscious decision of not throwing away your curiosity and exploration as a child; maintaining an open mind to explore and try new things; willingness to risk being unpopular as you pursue your dreams and ambitions; working smart and hard at whatever you set out to do; having clarity of who you truly are, your identity, what you truly want and its significance to you. Your life should be a life of increase and to leave everybody you come across with the impression of

increase. That is what you were wired to do. You should take full responsibility for your life, your actions and inactions. You have the potential so
why not explore this potential to the maximum? You were born for more
and should be true to your identity. Anything less is short changing you
and living below your potential. Stretch your abilities to the maximum and
you will be amazed about all that you are capable of doing in your life time.
Many times I pause to take stock of where I came from and what I have
achieved and accomplished and I am awestruck with what is possible when
we allow ourselves to do all that we are capable of doing.

Created in God's Image

> *"So God created human beings in his own image. In the image of God*
> *he created them; male and female he created them"*
> *~ The Bible*

One early morning while driving, the words "made in the image of
God" flashed through my mind. I got very excited about the thought of
being made in the image of the ever present, all knowing, all powerful, all
giving, abundant and opulent God. The more I reflected on my identity
as a reflection of the image of God, the more I started dreaming of all the
possibilities embedded in my heritage and identity. I asked myself whether
there is anything too difficult for me to achieve and the answer was a
definite 'No'. I questioned the limitations I have placed on myself and
all the lies I have bought into for many years. Right there I made up my
mind to use my identity and profound heritage to continue to achieve my
limitless potential, explore the possibilities, live the life I have imagined,
help you get what you want and the life you have dreamt about while living
a blazing trail of successes and accomplishments behind after completing
my earthly assignment, mission and calling.

Your Identity and Heritage are a Great Asset!

I was blown away by the fact that all I needed to be massively successful and live an amazing life was already in me. The thoughts of limitation,
competition, and self-denigration began to vanish, while thoughts of
limitless abundance, opulence, wellness, success, significance, and possibilities started flooding my whole being. Just think for a moment the fact that
you are a reflection of God's creative, spiritual, intelligent, communicative,
relational, and purposeful attributes. Let this thought sink in for a few
minutes. You are made in God's image and therefore you have the power to

have it all! You have it made and you should not go another day belittling, depreciating, criticizing and vilifying yourself. Doing that is an insult to the God who created you in His image. I have said to thousands of people who attend my seminars and talks that all that they need and ever will need to be successful is already available and within them. You need to stop looking elsewhere for answers and start looking within yourself. You hold the key to your present results and the key to massive results.

Made in the image of God confirms that you are a creative genius. You can create whatever you want through the power of your imagination. Most people use their imaginations to talk themselves into believing that they don't have what it takes and they are "turkeys" in the grand scheme of things. You have creative abilities and you can release those qualities to work for you. When you turn on your creative valves, you will begin to paint great pictures on the canvas of your mind and start taking massive actions on your ideas.

You are a creative genius!

There is no shortage of ideas but rather people with broken focus who are not using their creative abilities to problem solve, innovate, and create what is needed. You have abundance and riches in your creative mind. You have a 'gold mind', you have reservoirs of creative ideas, concepts, and life altering designs lying dormant within you. What you need is the awareness to tap into your creative vault to bring it out. It will serve you well to stop suggesting and convincing yourself that creativity only belongs to a select few. Your ability to navigate our complex but wonderful world is as a result of your creative genes and DNA. Tap into your creativity and help people get what they want. Use your creativity to solve business problems and lead your organization through change and transformation. Use your creativity to build a successful company, develop a cure for cancer, AIDS and other diseases under the caption 'terminal'; ignite a fire in your young mind; address human challenges; build a wellness business that helps people live better and longer lives. In you lies the solution to someone's problems. You have a solution to that business challenge. Why not tap into your creativity?

Your spirituality makes you unstoppable!

You are a spiritual being and understanding that makes you unstoppable. You are first and foremost a spiritual being; you live in a body and you have a soul. Being a spiritual being puts you on a creative plane as opposed to being on a competitive plane. Being a spiritual being says you always have help available whenever you need it. Your help is a prayer away. Prayer is about tapping into the divine and communicating with God. It is very easy to operate from our senses because that is what we are trained to do. When you operate from your senses you are limiting your capacity to grow and achieve. You are endowed with all the intelligence you need to be achieving massive success. Intelligence comes from the Latin verb *intellegere*, which means "to understand". Your intelligence is comprised of your acumen, aptitude, astuteness, brainpower and your capacity to have a successful life. Intelligence is the highest faculty of the mind and your capacity for comprehending general truths. You have the required intelligence to achieve whatever you put your mind to. Stop limiting yourself and start using your intelligence to do all that you and you only can do. You and you alone can do certain things and you have the intelligence to do it. You are still alive for the main reason of doing what you alone are called to do. There is not another you and there will never be another you in the history of humankind. Your assignment is cut out for you so go use your intelligence to be, do, have and contribute more.

Comprehending the full meaning of being created in the image of God should free you to go out and use your capacity and potential to the full. It is your right to live the life you have imagined and not be stopped by unfounded erroneous belief systems created by people to control and manipulate you for their own selfish reasons. You are pure potential and you should begin to see yourself that way and walk in your identify with the right self-image, self-esteem and self-concept. Nothing can stop you from realizing your potential unless you stop yourself. In my training and seminars I have the habit of asking people what they want and everybody has something to say about that. I have heard my participants and conference attendees say things like: I want a beautiful house, a successful business, a great career, a fantastic spouse or relationship, to become a CEO of a large corporation, and so on. I then follow-up with the next question; *what is stopping you then*? This is where I begin to hear excuses like: I don't have the education or the money, I am not in the right environment, I come from a poor family, and all the excuses that you have heard or read about yourself. Use your identity as the power to have it all. Relish in your identity and begin to dream large dreams because of who you are and whose image you represent. You are a person of significant value and don't you kid yourself thinking any less!

You are pure potential!

I was recently with a great friend of mine called Mark. He is an engineer by profession and has done very well in his career. He was going through a difficult season in his life. As we progressed in our conversation I realized that Mark, due to the current struggles in his life, had forgotten who he truly was, the successes he has had, the qualities he brought to the table, skills and gifts he had. He started degrading himself as not having what it takes to turn things around. I had to remind him of his track record, the successes he has had, his qualities of bringing people together for assignments, and his capacity to draw people to himself. I also reminded him of his identity and counseled him on being careful of how he looks at the world in times of adversity and challenge. At the end of the conversation Mark gave a smile, squared up, and walked confidently from our meeting with resolve, renewed energy, and the strength to turn things around and pursue his goals. You can turn things around when you begin to use your inner resources and strength to change your life. You have help available through your identity to make your life a masterpiece. Go back to your roots and remember you are made in God's image and therefore you have the qualities, potential, skills, and inner resources to make your life a masterpiece.

The True You is Extraordinary

"Make your lives a masterpiece; you only get one canvas."
~ E. A. Bucchianeri

A lot of people lack self-esteem and have poor self- image. They don't feel good about themselves based on what they have been told and what they believe to be true. These people pump themselves up by the kind of clothes they wear, the kind of car they drive, and the things they have and say. They pump themselves up to make them feel better about themselves because they really don't accept themselves as made in the image of God. Your value is not based on what people say about you or your limited thinking, nor is it based on your external circumstances. Your true value is in your identity and heritage. Quit telling yourself lies and refreshing the wrong stories about you; what people say about you, what the environment says about you. The real you is extraordinary and you have to begin to think that way. You are an amazing person created to do exceptional things in your lifetime. You have great intelligence and are wonderful in a lot of ways. However, you have created barriers in your mind based on life's experiences and challenges. Your experiences do not define you so use your challenges and experiences, as a data point, to refine you, and as a springboard for greater things. Your experiences are just a reflection of how far you have come, where you have been, and not a reflection of where you will be tomorrow unless you choose to live there.

Raymond Holliwell, in his book, 'Working with the Law' wrote, *"There is a marvelous inner world that exists within us, and the revelation of such a world enables us to do, to attain and to achieve anything we desire within the bounds or limits of Nature."* When you hold the thought of how extraordinary you are, how perfect your DNA is, you will achieve what you want. Failure in life is due in most part to focusing on your external results as opposed to focusing on changing your inner condition. Have a revelation of your marvelous inner world and use it to achieve massive success. Success in life is due to taking sides with what you are truly created to do. Steve Bow said, *"God's gift to us is more talent and ability than we'll ever hope to use in our lifetime. Our gift to God is to develop as much of that talent and ability as we can in this lifetime."*

You don't want to be copying someone else or living someone else's dreams. You have the ability, personality and experience required to run in your lane and fulfill your dreams. You were not born to be a photocopy but created to be an original. Stop spending your time looking back. You will never move forward if you're always looking in your rear view mirror. The past is past; yesterday is gone and will never again be repeated in the history of your life. You have a blank canvas presented to you every day to use in creating the life you want. You are the only one with the power to make your life beautiful. Be the poem you have dreamt of writing. Get involved in developing the movie of your life. You are the main character in this movie, so make it a great movie. Today you have the opportunity to move beyond negative self-talk and self-imposed limitation to design the life you want. You have the tools in shaping the life you have imagined so go out there and prove to yourself that is possible when you dare to try! Be true to yourself and start making each day extraordinary.

Embrace your uniqueness today

"Don't compare yourself with anyone in this world...
if you do so, you are insulting yourself."
~ Bill Gates

Here is a statement I want you to remember for the rest of your life, *"If you are still alive, your life matters."* Your birth is a statement in its own right, saying your life matters. Your uniqueness is what makes you different from everyone else. You are made up of your emotions, feelings, thoughts, behaviors and attitudes. You are not what people say you are, what people want you to be, but rather what you were born to be and accomplish. You are unique and there will never be another you. Deepak Chopra wrote, *"Each of us is a unique strand in the intricate web of life and here to make a contribution."* Steve Jobs came and changed our world and how we relate with computers and technology. There will never be another Steve Jobs. You are special in your own ways and your uniqueness is suited to do a specific thing. What are you suited for? I believe it's a big mistake to want to be like someone else. If you were meant to be like someone else you will not be you. I like the words of Ivan E. Coyote which says, *"I am a rare species, not a stereotype."* Embracing your uniqueness is the beginning of freedom and using your power to have it all. You are unique and exclusive. You are in a league of your own to live life the way you have imagined it. You are only one of a kind in the entire world so explore your uniqueness in the achievement of your dreams. A lot of people are copy cats and therefore are not able to be, do and have more, and achieve all their goals. Wanting to be someone else will create an inferiority complex and conflict in your mind. Why would you like to be a copy when you can be an original? Why not embrace your distinctiveness? You have a unique role to play in the universe and in the grand scheme of things. You might have significantly and positively impacted someone's life without even knowing it. Nobody can look at life through the exact same lenses as you do.

Your potential for growth and development is unlimited. Margaret Mead puts it beautifully; *"Always remember that you are absolutely unique. Just like everyone else."* The real you is the inner you, and when you are living with the real you, your life takes on greater meaning. Every stage of life has its inherent strengths. The stage of life you are in right now is meaningful even if it feels like you are stuck, in a rut, or spinning 'round and 'round. You have the power to shape your future using your unique attributes. You have the ability to influence Today is a new day. The only day you have control over is today. Today will never again be repeated in the history of your life so why waste it on what could have been, what might have been or what should have been. It is a day you have never seen before and will never see again. Stop telling yourself the lies of one day

I will do this or that. There is no 'one day'. Saying 'one day' to suit your inaction and excuses is false and self-defeating. Today is the day and this is the day you have. Use it and use it well. The lies of 'one day' has not taken you anywhere, never taken anybody anywhere, and will not take you anywhere in the future. So many people are selling themselves short in the name of 'one day I will do this or that'. Stop fooling yourself and start understanding the reality that today matters and that the sum total of your todays will make your tomorrow, which ultimately leads to your destiny. How many days have the lies of 'one day' stolen from you? Seize the greatness and uniqueness of today. Throughout today, you have an incredible amount of opportunity to move your life in the direction you want it to go.

Your possibilities are unlimited

Your creative power is unlimited. You have the ability and power to have it all. Your beliefs, the basis and source of your beliefs, will support or reject the statement that you have infinite possibilities available to you to fulfill your purpose and dreams. When you realize that the creative power in you is unlimited then there is no reason why you should be limiting the extent to which you should have and enjoy the life you have been given. When you draw from the infinite source of supply and provision you need not be afraid of taking more than your share of what is available to you. True wealth begins with our alignment with the God of abundance and opulence. Embracing a mindset of possibilities begins with an opulent thought pattern; the thought of increase and abundance without limits. Opulence is not only about money or financial resources. Opulence is largely about generosity and liberality. An opulent mindset or way of thinking is about the feeling that you possess various riches you can give to others, and giving liberally without limitation is what opens the door to more abundance in your life. When you develop the mindset of opulence, live like you believe it, and take concrete steps to truly live it, you open the way for greater supplies to flow in and through you. My parents gave me the name Gift and I took that literally, to always give to the charities of my choice and to friends and relations who might need my help. Anytime I go to the bank to send money I always say something light "God, thank you for the opportunity to give." I get a kick out of giving and I can tell you the more I give, the more I am excited about the opportunity to give. Giving is a spiritual law and I can narrate in great detail story after story of the blessings on my life which I know came from developing an abundant mentality and the heart of giving. I don't know about you but as for me and my business, we will continue to give!

When you refresh others, you are refreshed!

In His book the *Spirit of Opulence*, Judge Thomas J. Troward puts it this way, "*We are not called upon to give what we have not yet got and to run into debt; but we are to give liberally of what we have, with the knowledge that by so doing we are setting the law of circulation to work, and as this law brings us greater and greater inflows of every kind of good, so our out-giving will increase, not by depriving ourselves of any expansion of our own life that we may desire, but by finding that every expansion makes us the more powerful instruments for expanding the life of others. 'Live and let live' is the motto of the true opulence.*"

You have tremendous opportunity available to you. You are not in the current position or state because someone has taken what belongs to you or has monopolized the area you want to operate in. There is adequate need for your products and services. There is a need for your knowledge and skill. You are the solution to someone's problems and challenges. There is a market for what you do or are thinking of doing. The doors of opportunity are opening every single day. You have an abundance of opportunity, and no person should say that they are deprived of opportunity. The tide of opportunity comes along every single day. You are either flowing with the tide through your openness to opportunity or swimming away from the tide due to your lack of openness to change and not being in harmony with the laws of nature. Remember that no one is kept in lack or poverty by scarcity in the supply of resources. There is more abundance and will remain more abundance after you have had your share. There is no limit to what you can do, have, or achieve in your lifetime. There is no limit to the supply of what you will require to fulfill your ambition, dreams and vision. There is no limit to the supply of the resources we need in the fulfilment of our earthly assignment. Remember, there is enough to go around and there will always be enough after you have had your share. What you need to tap into the opportunity is learning to do things a certain way. Unlimited possibilities are available to you when you seek out these possibilities. Your life is filled with opportunities and possibilities. There are countless stories of people you know and I know who came from a place of nothing or barely surviving and have amassed significant wealth and resources to do all the things they want in life. They started from nothing, only with a consuming passion to help others get what they want and an idea to turn their lives around. You may wonder whether you are a candidate for greatness; the answer is a resounding yes! Live in an atmosphere of expectation and use the power of your imagination to move the needle of success and accomplishment in your favor. Pablo Valle said, "*Write it down, my life is filled with unlimited possibilities.*" You should try writing each morning when you wake up and each evening before you retire to bed that my life is filled with unlimited possibilities. Repeat this to yourself over and over again until it sinks deep in your subconscious mind. This is a fact and the truth and you better believe it at the cellular level. Thomas Edison puts it in a nice way, "When you have exhausted all possibilities remember this, you haven't." What a great way to look at all the possibilities around you and in you.

ACTION EXERCISES FOR MASSIVE SUCCESS

1. Write down what 'made in the image of God' means to you.

2. How will you use the revelation of your identity made in God's image for massive success?

3. Make a list of your talents and how you are going to use them to achieve extraordinary accomplishments.

4. Your potential is unlimited and your possibilities are enormous. List three things you will do with your potential to achieve massive success.

5. Write down 4 actions you will take immediately to leverage your identity and heritage to achieve maximum results.

Chapter Two

Habits for Massive Success

Dr. Phil, on his TV show, said that "LIFE REWARDS ACTION." And Tony Robbins frequently says "TAKE MASSIVE ACTION." Why are people afraid of taking massive action? Some of the reasons include fear, laziness, procrastination, the lack of a sense of urgency, being satisfied with the current results, lack of discipline, lack of commitment, not being accountable, and others. Is massive success for you? Absolutely yes if you really want it, are prepared to do what massively successful people do, ready to put in the work, and to develop the mental toughness required, shift your paradigms and do whatever it will take. You cannot be doing the same thing over and over again and expect a different result. Here is a sneak peek of what massive success folks do:

Intense capacity for focus

People who have massive success have intense focus, put emphasis on what they want, give energy and attention to what's most important, and concentrate single-mindedly on their goals and actions. The Law of focus states that whatever we dwell upon grows. We get more of what we focus on. The things we focus on become our reality. The more we think about something, the more it becomes part of our reality.

Think maximum achievement and success

Massively successful people align their thoughts, emotions and actions with maximum achievement and success habits; they eliminate from their lives anything and all the things not in consonance with where they are headed. They think big and take the necessary action in tandem with that.

Continuous self-introspection and continuous improvement

Massively successful people have self-awareness; they know their strengths and challenges, how to manage these challenges, and have developed the habit of leveraging their strength. They also make continuous improvement in their daily routine.

Controlled Emotions

There are times when the going gets tough, times when you are under the weather and when things don't go the way you have planned and envisaged. Massively successful people have the same conditions and go through similar emotional challenges but have developed self-control. They bring their emotions under control and do what they need to do in spite of vacillating emotions.

Immense collaboration

Each one needs all of us! Massively successful people believe in the principle of leverage, mastermind, and the importance of collaboration to achieve results. They forge alliances for maximum performance and an intense desire for collaboration.

Significant Self Confidence

Self-confidence is the food of champions. Massively successful people believe in themselves to the point that they are sometimes construed as arrogant. Self-confidence says you know beyond any reasonable doubt that you have what it takes and what you need to achieve the success you want.

Coachable attitude

Massively successful people have a coachable attitude and are not afraid to ask for help. When they see something that will add value to their lives and where they want to go, they quickly seek out help from those ahead of them and learn from the masters.

Know precisely what they want

The first step to massive success is to precisely know what you want. Understand what you have to give to get what you want, be ready to pay the price and invest in what you want, and go after it with gusto! Massively successful individuals can tell you, in detail, about what they want.

Operate from a position of abundance and opulence

Massively successful people believe in the principle of abundance and opulence. They are generous and give with liberality. They have an abundant mentality and are never afraid to be more, achieve more, give more, and live the true life of abundance. They leave everybody they encounter with an impression of increase.

Life-long personal development

Those who are massively successful are life-long learners. They invest significantly in personal development to continue to be the best, be relevant and bring significant value to the marketplace. They never stop learning because they know that there is always room for improvement and value addition.

Thinks independently

Massively successful individuals are confronted with so much information, just like anybody else; information from media, bosses, co-workers, friends, and centres of influence; however, they think on purpose and intentionally in alignment with what will best serve their interests.

Open to change and transformation

Massively successful people believe in personal change and transformation. They know that for things to change they have to change. They are open to change when required, are flexible with the changing times, embrace new technology and inventions, and adapt to the changing times.

Great Givers

Massively successful people believe in giving. They believe that there is more than enough to go around. They know that for the free flow of increase in their lives, giving is the key. They get a kick out of giving, and love the whole idea of giving their time, treasure, and talent to those who need it.

Ensure win-win outcomes for all

Massively successful individuals believe in a win-win outcome from their interactions and business deals. They know that when they win and the other party also wins, it opens more doors for repeat business and long-lasting relationships. They believe that together, everyone achieves more!

Pursue balanced lifestyle

Massively successful people believe that a balanced lifestyle is what brings longevity, health and wellness, successful relationships, peace of mind, financial freedom, social connections, and great self-image, self-concept and self-esteem.

Great believers in honesty

Massively successful people practice honesty as a virtue and believe that the laws of the universe come into play with honesty. They know that honesty frees their mind to be creative and innovative, and to focus on abundance and opulent-thinking patterns.

ACTION EXERCISES FOR MASSIVE SUCCESS

1. Make a list of massive success habits you already have.

2. Identify four habits you want to start developing right away.

3. Decide and commit to use those habits for maximum achievement.

4. Look for an accountability partner to help you anchor these habits.

5. Ensure that you consciously use your new habits in your daily routine.

Chapter Three

Diamond in the Rough

Think like a masterpiece

You are created a masterpiece; if you don't get it, read the statement one more time. You are a masterpiece created in God's image. You should learn to think like a masterpiece. The thoughts you think determines your words, your words determine your feelings and attitudes, your feelings determine your actions, and your actions determine your results. Thinking a certain way has a reflection on your current results. To think like a masterpiece is to replace limited thinking with possibility thinking. Masterpiece thinking is about filling your mind with the right thoughts, meditating on things that are true, noble, reputable, authentic, compelling and courteous. The best, not the worst; beautiful not ugly; blessing not cursing. Thinking like this creates excellence in you and positions you to attract good into your life. It is vital to think like a masterpiece if you are going to use your inner power to have it all. To think like a masterpiece means you don't accept whatever you read. You are an intelligent person and you have to draw your own conclusions from what you read. You have to be an independent thinker who will think for yourself and not go with the crowd. The crowd or majority can be sincere, but sincerely wrong. Be independent in your thinking, evaluate whatever you read, and check it to ensure that it is in alignment with your values, beliefs and where you are headed in life. Most people tend to believe what the majority think and feel strongly about, but thinking like a masterpiece is to think independently of all others. Some people don't think at all and hence the mess in their lives. They allow any thought to flow rampant in their minds and most of those thoughts are negative in nature. When you use your thinking to create, to change something and to help solve people's problems, you will be rewarded big time. After many years of training and conducting seminars, I came to the conclusion that most people don't intentionally think about the direction of their lives. It's a small wonder; they are just surviving when they should be thriving.

Thinking like a masterpiece also means you think outside the box, continuously improve, and are creative and innovative. The future belongs to those who are always looking for new ways of improving people's lives and the world around them. The person who is committed to improving lives and making the world a better place will never lack any good thing. No good thing will be withheld from you when you use your mind to create solutions and think of making things better and not worse. Someone said you are either solving problems or creating problems. Where do you stand? Masterpiece thinking requires purposeful thinking, without it you may find that you are vacillating based on whatever or whoever is able to give you instant gratification. Develop the discipline of possibility thinking in everything you do. When you encounter negativity in a situation you are dealing with, make it a habit to start with possibility because if you believe, all things are possible. Learn to think like an artist. It will open your creative and imaginative mind to paint creative pictures on the canvass of your mind and create the movie of your life. You sure can create a great movie of your life where all the things you want fall into place. You have the power to have it all! Stop short-changing yourself. Masterpiece thinking creates room for your talent to flourish and helps you achieve extraordinary results.

Let go of all excuses

"Ninety-nine percent of the failures come from
people who have the habit of making excuses."
~ *George Washington Carver*

Making excuses is a deadly disease. It eats away your future and steals your tomorrow like cancer. Excuses slowly eat away your future and well-being. Most of the struggles, poverty, and failures we see today are a result of people making excuses. You may know and have come across some of those people who thrive on excuses. I still meet people using excuses I used years ago and let go because I know better. It is like as I let go of excuses, others are finding them and using them. One of the excuses I used for many years was that I am not ready to do the things I wanted to do. I kept myself hidden for years, telling myself it was not yet the right time. I literally did not go out there using my talents because I convinced myself that I was not ready and that I needed more time. After training and speaking for years, I have had people come to me after my presentations to ask if I had a book they could buy or when was I going to put my ideas and experiences into a book. I always responded with the statement "At the right time." I gave this reason for years because I made myself believe that it was not the right time. I came to realize there is never a right time. Excuses are stealing and eating away your future one excuse at a time. Excuses will not change your current condition as long as you continue to feed them. Excuses fed will continue to grow big into a monster. The more you give yourself excuses, the more you begin to believe those excuses as legitimate and normal. Excuses may give you a feel-good and a justification for inaction.

Jack Canfield, the billionaire co-author of *Chicken Soup for the Soul* said, "*One of life's fundamental truths states, 'Ask and you shall receive.' As kids we get used to asking for things, but somehow we lose this ability in adulthood. We come up with all sorts of excuses and reasons to avoid any possibility of criticism or rejection.*" Excuses will help you explain away and justify your current state but will never help you change the state. Excuses will create room for you to put the blame of inaction on someone or something else and not on yourself. Excuses will not inspire you to action. Your present position and condition in life is a result of all the excuses you have made, as well as your inactions. Mark Twain said, "*There are a thousand excuses for failure but never a good reason.*" Anytime you make excuses you are handing over the control of your life to outside forces; you shift your mindset from going after your dreams to 'one day I will do it'. Making excuses becomes a habit and, before you know it, you are jumping from one excuse to the next instead of facing challenges and finding ways to work through or around those challenges.

Excuses are stealing and eating away your future one excuse at a time!

Why are you not achieving your goals and fulfilling your mission in life? Why are you not as successful as you wish to be? Is it a lack of training or education? Did other people just have better opportunities or lucky breaks than you had? For things to change you have to stop coming up with justification for your current state and take full responsibility for your actions. It's not about the conditions you find yourself in, because others have had the same conditions and have been very successful. It is like kids from the same family who had the same opportunity to grow and develop, yet after a certain age, some become successful, others are just surviving, and others are living a life of poverty. It is, therefore, not the conditions, but rather taking action and disciplining yourself to do the things you have to do that separates the achievers from those getting by. When you eliminate the need to explain your shortcomings or failures, you'll come alive and awaken your dreams! In his book *Excuses be Gone*, Dr. Wayne Dyer provided the following excuses people give for inaction. If any of these excuses apply to you then do something about it. Some of the excuses include: "…it will be difficult, it's going to be risky, it will take a long time, I don't deserve it, I can't afford it, it's not in my nature, no one will help me, it has never happened before, I am not strong enough, I am not smart enough, I am too old or not old enough, the rules won't let me, it's too big, I don't have the energy, it's in my personal history, I am too busy, I am too scared." What are your excuses? Spend a few minutes and reflect on your personal excuses. The following questions should help you in your reflection: what excuses are holding you back? Is the excuse true or a figment of your imagination? Where did the excuse come from? What are you getting as a result of the excuse or what purpose is the excuse serving? How will your life be different if you let go these excuses? If you were to do all the things you wanted to do without excuses, what will the movie of your life look like?

Newton's First Law of Motion states that a body at rest will remain at rest unless an outside force acts on it, and a body in motion at a constant velocity will remain in motion in a straight line unless acted upon by an outside force. When you act on your excuses and let go of those excuses, you begin a life of freedom and start to use your inner powers and resources to achieve your goals and fulfil your potential.

"Often, when we are about to break out of our comfort zone,
we experience fear, and that is a non-resourceful state,
because it blocks us from achieving results."
~ Unknown

Tony Robins teaches that as humans we need to feel safe, and sometimes when we push ourselves out of our comfort zone, we leave the state of certainty – and it can get uncomfortable. We ask ourselves questions like: Am I going to be able to do this? What if I get hurt? What if I embarrass myself? But we also thrive when we have a challenge in our life, and we want to find a way to dance in between certainty and uncertainty. The person with no excuses is the one who will rise, evolve, develop, and grow into the person they were destined to be. The benefits of letting go of excuses includes: you can now create the movie of your life being success-ful, living the life you have imagined; running that successful business, having the financial freedom to do all the things you want to do without thinking about money, providing for your family with a lot more left to give, and being available to make a contribution to causes you believe in.

You have greatness in you

"Some are born great, some achieve greatness, and
some have greatness thrust upon them."
~ William Shakespeare

Most people underestimate the power of their dreams and the influ-ence they will have should they allow the power of the human spirit to flourish. Each one of us has greatness within us and this is the time to bring your greatness to the forefront. You may encounter challenges and adversity on the path to unleash the power within you but it is the challenges and adversities that lead to greatness. Nurture and grow yourself because greatness and success is what you attract by the person you become. You first be, and then success and a life of significance will follow. Choose the right friends and surround yourself with the people who can encourage you and challenge you to become what you have set your mind upon. Always challenge yourself to go beyond your comfort zone and continually invest in the development of your skills. Read, study, practice and teach what you have leant, for with practice and teaching you continue to hone your skills. Set stretch goals that cause you to explore your potential and hidden talents. Until the rubber band is stretched we can never know how far it will go. Until you stretch yourself to the maximum you can never know all the things you can achieve in your lifetime. Develop the movie of the life you want and visualize you having achieved it. Expand your vision, sharpen your skills, and put in the time to make your dream come true. Resolve that in the upcoming week, month or year you will exceed your goals and take the necessary action for that to happen.

You are a gift to the world so be the gift and act in alignment with that belief. All your life experiences, good and bad, can all be used for inspiring others for action, personal growth and development. I use most of my life stories in my speeches and seminars. Recently I was speaking to a group of people who were in the process of having their company divested. Some of the people have worked in the company for thirty years. I was speaking to them about change and resilience and how to re-energize, think different, and position themselves to explore the changes ahead. I narrated my life stories and experiences through change and transformation. I got an email from a few of them saying, "Please keep telling your stories, I finally got it." Another said, "Your stories inspired me to look at change differently," and others said, "You brought back hope and what we needed to do at this time to be resilient through the tough times." Your life stories – the good, the bad, and the ugly – will serve a purpose. Regardless of what is going on around you, be thankful that you are still alive and well. Within you are new ideas and more skills than you will ever use in your lifetime. You have a calling, a mission, or an assignment that you are uniquely qualified to deliver. Don't die with your ideas and cheat the world out of your contribution.

> *You are a gift to the world, so be the gift and*
> *act in alignment with that belief!*

"Believe in yourself" as Norman Vincent Pearl said in his book *The Power of Positive Thinking*. Believing in yourself has become a cliché but when you think deeply about the statement you will begin to comprehend the power and efficacy of the statement. Until you believe that you have the power to have it all, or that your skills are needed to solve someone's problems, until you believe that you have the seed of greatness inside you, you may not go after your dreams with gusto. Trust in your ideas, have faith, strengthen your abilities and use your talents in achieving your goals. Your mission is achievable so don't talk yourself out of it. Silence the negative voices and forge ahead. There comes a time when you have to tell the voices that are saying, "You can't do this, you are not qualified for this, you don't have the money or the right talent" to just SHUT UP. Create a larger vision for your life because the larger the vision, the more it stretches you. Unleash the power in you for greatness. Stop the excuses and the procrastination and get fired up and move ahead. You have the ability to step into the life that you have always imagined and design the life you want. Become unstoppable, set your mind on what you want to achieve, be tenacious in reaching your goals, and don't let anyone talk you out of your dreams. Keep working your plan for when you work it, it will work. You are a miracle about to happen! So dare to live above the opinions of other people. Follow your heart. Live your own life, and don't live someone else's dream of you. Use your challenges and stumbling blocks as stepping stones to greatness. You are bigger than any of the problems you face. Look around, and you'll find opportunities silently waiting for you. You have the seed of greatness within you, so don't squander or diminish it!

Action Exercises for Massive Success

1. What does it mean to think like a masterpiece?

2. Come up with 4 characteristics of masterpiece thinking and how you will use it personally.

3. Make a list of all your excuses and write beside each excuse how it is limiting you and how it is serving you.

4. Identify 3 excuses you will stop making immediately.

5. You have greatness in you, so how are you going leverage your greatness to achieve massive success?

Chapter Four

The Gift of Adversity

Adversity will refine you, then build you!

John Maxwell, the leadership guru, expressed his understanding of adversity in the following words, "*The trials and pressures of life and how we face them often define us. Confronted by adversity, many people give up while others rise up. How do those who succeed do it? They persevere. They find the benefit to them personally that comes from any trial. And they recognize that the best thing about adversity is coming out on the other side of it. There is sweetness to overcoming your troubles and finding something good in the process, however small it may be. Giving up when adversity threatens can make a person bitter. Persevering through adversity makes one better.*" Why is it that some people fall under the weight of adversity and give up while others rise and thrive with adversity? Those who persevere through adversity become stronger, wiser, more determined, and inspired to leave their mark on the annals of history. I don't know about you, but I have had my own share of adversity. I made it through the tough times and you can too.

During my challenging school years, I walked several kilometers to the university I attended at the time because I did not have the money to pay for public transport. I used those long walks to think about life and success. Several times I had to eat my lunch in the morning because I would get so hungry after the long walks. I washed the dishes at the university cafeteria after my mates had finished eating. These were interesting and challenging times. There were several times I thought and wished I could just sit at the cafeteria and eat just like all the others, but I did not have the money. I made it through the challenges successfully and I can tell you that whatever it is that you may be going through, remember "This too shall pass". Adversity will always come at some point in your life; allow it to refine you, build you up, and help you develop the mental toughness and tenacity to reach your goal and fulfil your potential.

Don't waste your pain

> *"Pain is just temporary; if you give up it becomes eternal."*
> *~ Dexter Lim*

While pursuing my master's degree and struggling to make ends meet, I remember on one occasion I had to go to the University for an exam. All I had on me was a one way train ticket to go and write the exam. I finished the exam and boarded the train to return home but this time without a ticket. Somewhere in the middle of the journey, an officer approached me and requested to see my ticket to which I responded I don't have one and pleaded for mercy. I believe the officer was in a very bad mood that day or perhaps he was just doing his duty. When the train arrived at the next station, the officer threw me out. I was very embarrassed with the ordeal, shed a few tears, and was scared because I was in the middle of nowhere wondering how I was going to get back home. It was a very painful experience. I wondered why life was this way. I asked several questions, wondering why me and whether there were others going through similar experiences. I felt alone and afraid. These were the days when there were no cell phones to call and ask for help. I waited several hours and got back on the next available train, but this time on the look-out for any person resembling an officer. I finally got home and promised myself never to allow this experience to be repeated in my life. This was a defining moment, the day that changed my life and intensified my quest and search for a life of success and achievement. Out of this pain and experience I resolved to pursue my goals with gusto, to never give up on my dreams, to keep looking for ways to make it in life like the others I have admired on the streets of London. I worked part time in a Persian Carpet store lifting heavy carpets with customers coming in to look at different carpets. For whatever reason, each time we had packed all the carpets neatly and was about to close for the day, a customer would walk in and we had to bring down all the carpets the customer was interested in looking at. Most of the time these customers left without buying any carpet and that felt like a waste of time. It was tough but an interesting chapter in my life. I got to learn about different carpets from Iran, Iraq, and other Arab states, and the type of carpets used by the rich and the famous in the Arab world. When life gives you a lemon just use it!

No experience is ever wasted!

What is your pain? What are you going through on your path to success? What are the discouraging episodes in your life? Turn your pain into an asset and let it motivate, inspire and propel you into finding your niche in life. There are those who crash under the weight of pain; let this not be you. Don't waste your pain.

Les Brown had his share of adversity too. Leslie Calvin Brown and his twin brother, Wesley, were born on February 17, 1945, on the floor of an abandoned building in Liberty City, a low-income section of Miami, Florida. At six weeks of age, both boys were adopted by Mamie Brown, a 38-year cafeteria cook and domestic worker. Les' adopted mother had confidence in him and believed that this boy was capable of doing great things. Les' teachers did not share these sentiments though. As a child, Les found excitement in typical boyhood misadventures. He liked to have fun, and he liked attention. Overactive and mischievous, Les was a poor student because he was unable to concentrate, especially in reading. His restlessness and inattentiveness, coupled with his teachers' insufficient insight into his true capabilities, resulted in his being labeled "educable mentally retarded" in the fifth grade. It was a label he found hard to remove, in large part because he did not try. "They said I was slow so I held to that pace," he recounted in his book. Despite the lack of self-esteem and low confidence this created, he learned how to reach his full potential with the encouragement of his mother and assistance by a helpful teacher in high school. This became a key point in many of Les' motivational speeches. While in high school, Les used to fantasize about being onstage speaking to thousands of people, and he recounted, "I used to write on pieces of paper, 'I am the world's greatest orator.'" Les met LeRoy Washington, a speech and drama instructor at Booker T. Washington High School in Miami where he truly learned about the sound and power of eloquent speech to stir and motivate people to action. On one occasion, Les told Washington in class that he couldn't perform a task because he was educable mentally retarded, to which the instructor responded, "Do Not Ever Say That Again! Someone's opinion of you does not have to become your reality." Those words provided Les liberation from his debilitating label.

Les got a job after high school as a city sanitation worker. He was determined to achieve his goal by pursuing a career in radio broadcasting. He had been captivated throughout his life with music and disc jockeys, so he repeatedly asked the owner of a local radio station about a position until the owner relented. Having no experience, Les was hired to perform odd jobs. Firmly intent on becoming a deejay, he learned all he could about the workings of a radio station. One day, when a disc jockey became drunk on the air and Les was the only other person at the station, he filled in at the microphone. The owner of the station was impressed with Les' performance and promoted him to part-time and then full-time disc jockey. Les moved to Columbus, Ohio in the late 1960's where he had a top-rated radio program, and was eventually given added duties as broadcast manager. He became more socially conscious and more of an activist, urging his listeners to political action. Part of the motivation behind this fervor came from Mike Williams, the station's news director and an activist who would eventually oversee Les' motivational speaking tours and programs. "I thought he was a master communicator," Williams told Cheryl Lavin of the Chicago Tribune. "I knew it was a gift. I saw him as an international figure. I saw him in very large situations, moving audiences." Les was fired by the radio station after he became too controversial with his radio messages.

Don't waste adversities, just use them!

In 1986, Les was broke and sleeping on the cold linoleum floor of his office, when he began to pursue a career as a motivational speaker. By the early 1990s, he was one of the highest paid speakers in the nation. His company, Les Brown Unlimited, Inc., earned millions of dollars a year from his speaking tours and the sale of motivational tapes and materials. Les' audience ranges from Fortune 500 companies to automobile workers to prison inmates to special-education classes to ordinary individuals. His mission is to "get a message out that will help people become uncomfortable with their mediocrity," he explained to a reporter for Ebony magazine. "A lot of people are content with their discontent. I want to be a catalyst to enable them to see themselves having more and achieving more." Les overcame his challenges and goes around the world to inspire people to live their dreams.

He is accredited with the following words, "You have greatness in you", and "You must be hungry" and other inspiring messages.

I remember attending a Get Motivated conference where Les was scheduled to speak. Thousands of people were waiting to hear Les speak. People came from far and wide, traveling hours just to hear Les speak into their lives. There was excitement in the air as the time drew close for Les' segment of the program. You can feel and sense the disappointment when it was announced later in the day that Les was not going to make it due to ill health. A number of people left immediately because all they came for was to hear Les Brown. Les has moved from adversity to triumph and used the mess he was in at one point to be his message. He never wasted the pain of his childhood but uses it to help others realize that you can use your pain for the greater good rather than allowing your pain to use you. Don't fall under the weight of your pain; don't waste your pain and the challenging stories of your life. Someone needs to hear your story, your struggles and how you came through the difficult times. Your story could be what someone needs to get up and get moving again.

A number of years ago actor Michael Douglas announced his battle with throat cancer during his appearance on *The David Letterman Show.* In spite of his battle with cancer he remained optimistic during this time of adversity and inspired others to look at the bright side of life. Going through adversity is tough but when all is said and done we come out stronger on the other side. When the going gets tough, when your world seems to be falling apart, when your business is about to close because you cannot meet your obligations, when you are fired from your job, when adversity hits you like a ton of bricks, when the rubber meets the road, what will you describe yourself as? Are you tough enough and having the tenacity and mental toughness to keep on keeping on in spite of all the difficulties? What lies at the very core of your character? You know how strong you are through adversity. You know what you are made of when you are in the midst of the storm. What you are on the outside is a reflection of what is happening on the inside. You cannot be any different from who you are on the inside.

Better but not bitter

"Either your troubles make you better, or they make you bitter.
We must always examine what's going on in our hearts."
~ Author TD Jakes

Life is not fair, as people say but God is good! Each one of us will have problems, challenges, obstacles and hurts that will cause us to either be bitter or better. Some grow up through the challenges while others give up. Challenges will either cause you to pursue your goals and dreams or make you give up. You have a choice which path you want to take. You have to decide how you are going to respond to the tough times life brings you and how you go through it. Charles R. Swindoll said, "*We cannot change our past... we cannot change the fact that people will act in a certain way. We cannot change the inevitable. The only thing we can do is play on the one string we have, and that is our attitude. I am convinced that life is 10% what happens to me and 90% of how I react to it. And so it is with you... we are in charge of our Attitudes.*" Going through tough times is what happens to all of us; however, what happens to us is not nearly as important as what happens in us.

My father was a building contractor and was blessed to work on some neat and large building contracts. After a while, he was no longer getting contracts so he decided to take on other businesses which did not perform as well as planned. My dad heard of an investment opportunity where the company promised huge return on his investment. Lured by the returns, he withdrew a significant amount of his retirement money and invested it in this so-called investment opportunity. Having received a certain return on the investment, he convinced my mother to also invest in the business. After a short while they lost all their investment. It was a scheme to collect people's money, give a reasonable return on investment to show that the scheme was working until they got a critical mass. The people who started the investment left the country with all the investment. Mum and Dad lost all their retirement benefits. Dad was very upset for a period of time and realized that there was nothing he could do to get his money back so holding onto the pain was a waste of time. We were afraid at the time that the experience of the loss would eventually kill Dad but he survived through the experience to tell the story of how not to be lured by highly inflated return-on-investment or too-good-to-be true schemes. Dad decided to let go and think outside the box. He forgave the crooks, put himself together, and got into small businesses to keep busy for some time. Dad had to let go in order to see other opportunities. I am suggesting you do what my dad did; forgive, calm down, let go, and have a clear head to see beyond the challenges. There are and always will be opportunities when you position yourself mentally to see it. It was Josh Shipp who said,

"*You either get bitter or you get better. It's that simple. You either take what has been dealt to you and allow it to make you a better person, or you allow it to tear you down. The choice does not belong to fate, it belongs to you*" It is important not to allow hurt to linger for a long time; let go and move on. Our natural inclination or default drive is to hold onto pain and disappointment, but that will be detrimental to your wellbeing and drive you nuts. Free your mind from the pain, learn from the experience, and move on.

What have you been dealt with? What are you holding onto and refusing to let go of? Who are you holding onto, thinking that letting go may be interpreted as a weakness? You will always win when you take the higher road. Someone said, "Refusal to let go is like allowing someone to occupy your mind rent free." I thought that was a great way to put it. You control your mind and you should decide who you keep in your mind and who you should let go of. I recently wrote an article titled, "The Gift of Good-bye". Little did I know that a significant number of people I knew in this particular organization had issues with letting go. The responses I received from a number of people were very humbling and also revealing. So many people are holding onto things and issues they have no business clinging to. I trust that you are not one of those people, holding onto bitterness because of a failed business, relationship, experience or something someone did to you. Don't waste your energy. It takes too much energy to hold onto the wrong stuff, especially issues that challenge and impact your emotions and feeling negatively. Simply put, "Be better, not bitter". I read this proverb but can't remember where I got it. It says "*Instead of complaining that the rose bush is full of thorns, be happy the thorn bush has roses.*" Get rid of all bitterness, rage and anger. You will live longer being a positive, possibility, gracious and focused person whose primary objective is leaving the world a better place than you found it! Make the choice to get rid of all bitterness so you can live a life of freedom!

Adversity is the food of champions

People naturally tend toward inertia. That's why self-improvement is such a struggle. But that's also why adversity lies at the heart of every success. The process of achievement comes through repeated failures and the constant struggle to climb to a higher level.
~ John C. Maxwell

Adversity lies at the heart of every success!

According to John Maxwell in his book *Sometimes You Win, Sometimes You Learn*, he mentioned that, "*Adversity can signal a coming positive transition if we respond correctly to it.*" We don't always have to see adversity as a negative all the time. Adversity can be a great teacher and a revealer of character and who we are at the very core. The obstacles we encounter each day can act as a springboard to greater things life has to offer. We gain experience through adversity if we care to look beyond the struggle. Some adversity we bring on ourselves without doing the due diligence before entering into a business, others are caused by people we trust. Others we will say that is life. Through adversity, we will either succeed or fail. When we respond to adversity in a positive manner we have the opportunity to grow from it or sink with it. Any time we react negatively in adversity we get more of the same. It's like the person who leaves one bitter relationship into the next and the next. We get more of what we focused on!"

The story of Brian Tracy and his success captures how you can turn adversity into something positive and make the best of what life throws at you. He, like all others, has had his share of adversity. I have read a significant number of the books written by Brian Tracy, invested in many of his audio programs, and had coaching from Focalpoint. He is one of the people who have inspired me to invest in personal development, do more, be more, and live a life of success.

Here is an abridged version of Brain Tracy's story as shared by Tom Butler-Bowden. "*Brian Tracy was born on January 5, 1944 in Charlotte-town, Prince Edward Island in Canada. Brian grew up in a poor family and had to wear charity store clothes. After dropping out of school he worked in a succession of laboring jobs, living in boarding houses. At 21 he found work on a Norwegian freighter ship and travelled around the world, but two years later was back laboring and doing some commission selling. Though not an outward success, Brian had always been interested in the question, 'What makes some people successful and others not?' As a freshly minted salesman, he started to read voraciously on selling techniques and what makes the best salespeople the best. He copied what they did, and slowly, his results improved. Six months later, he was the top salesperson in his company.*"

"*When he moved into management, he read everything he could find on managing people and built a large sales organization across several countries. Entering the real estate industry, he 'hit the books again' and talked to successful developers. His first project was financing, building and leasing out a three-million dollar shopping center. At night Tracy completed a high school diploma, and eventually gained entry to an MBA program to study business theory and marketing, which enabled him to become a management consultant. To learn about happiness, he read what he could find on metaphysics, psychology and motivation, and when he married, learned all he could about parenting. To get a sense of perspective, and find out why some countries were rich and others poor, he read widely on history, economics and politics.*"

"*After two decades of thinking about the question, 'What makes some people more successful than others?' Tracy decided to put everything he knew into a 'success system' which could help others. He designed a seminar, but it took about three years to really catch on. Then he released an audiotape program,* The Psychology of Achievement, *which went on to sell half a million copies. I have read* The Psychology of Achievement *so many times and each time I discover something new. This book ignited a passion in me and continues to inspire and enthused me anytime I read and study the contents of the book. Brian could have decided to quit and give up in light of all the struggles and challenges he had; instead he read books to find out why some people are more successful than others and what they actually did. Getting the answer to the question, he modeled the behavior of these successful people and became very successful as well. Brian says success is a learnable skill and if you learn and study what successful people do, you will be successful as well.*"

To achieve your goals and fulfil your potential, adversity, challenges and problems are part and parcel of experiences along the way. Get used to adversity and change, work through what life throws at you and you will surely achieve your goals. This is not to say that it will be easy, I am saying it will be worth it in the end. Here are a few things champions know about adversity. They know that adversity is the secret of champions, having the right mindset is crucial, working through personal challenges is a must, developing mental toughness is key, having faith to know that this too shall pass carries you through the difficult seasons, focusing on your goals, and keeping your dreams front and center are all ingredients for success.

Adversity will write and capture the movie of your life, and it is your response to adversity that will make your movie worthwhile. Fear in adversity will stop you from doing the things you want to do. Fear steals your energy, makes you apprehensive and doubtful, and takes away your joy. Fear causes you to feel out of control and make you vacillate on your decisions. Faith, on the other hand, says you are stronger than you think. Faith inspires you to keep on keeping on in spite of the storm. Faith is the assurance that the storm and adversity will pass. Faith keeps you steady and hopeful in the midst of adversity. Faith says it is well and it's just a matter of time. Choose faith, not fear.

During times of adversity, we forget that we have options. Allow the concept of 'next' to work for you. When one door closes, remember that there is another door about to open. Even if a door does not open immediately, a window may bring in fresh air to set things up for your comeback! During times of adversity you may feel lost in the heat, but don't allow that to happen. Your mind may be foggy at first but clear your mind as soon as you possibly can. Grieve if you must but don't allow the grieving process to persist for too long. Rest if you must but don't make resting your preoccupation. Allow each step of success, no matter how small it is, to energize and inspire you to dream on and move on. At times, dark clouds are a sign of an abundance of rain! Let the clouds be the sign that the tough times will not last. Your dark cloud could just be a word of encouragement, a little breakthrough, an open door or window of opportunity, and so forth. Let the clouds remind you that help is on the way and you can be on your feet again. Let the clouds build your hope that the current drought is about to end and there is light at the end of the tunnel. Life is about learning to work through adversity. When you do, you will be a different person from when you first got in. It's all a matter of perspective and the choices you make in the midst of adversity will either make you or break you. Use adversity and not let it use you!

My Share of Adversity

I entered into partnership with my buddy in a wellness and restaurant business. He was a professional chef with significant years of experience in the hotel industry. We invested in a property in a great location on a hill overseeing the city. It was a beautiful site in the evening when all the patrons came around. On one side of the property we had a squash court, a sauna, massage rooms and a recreational area. After work and on weekends the place was filled with professionals from various businesses and segments of society having a great time at our business place. On the other side of the property were the restaurant, two bar areas with pool tables, table tennis and a place to watch various movies on a wide screen. Folks just loved to visit this place to meet their business associates, friends and family. Others come to rent the facility for corporate functions, parties, training and other events. The business did very well until I discovered that my partner had been taking money out of the business without accounting for it. As the person managing the place, he felt he had the liberty to be generous with money for himself and his family, even though we made provision for his upkeep. Long story short, I lost all my investment and got out of the business. The situation created animosity between my buddy and I for a long time. I had the choice of being bitter over the ordeal but decided to take the higher road to let it go. It was not easy at first because I saw this investment as one of my strategies for multiple streams of income. But I forgave my buddy, learned from the experience and moved on. On the positive side I learned what works with clients, tested a number of principles for service excellence, and made a few friends from our pool of patrons. The experience made me better, not bitter.

I don't know about your experience with partnerships but if yours didn't work either, you sure have learnt a few lessons as well. There is something about taking the higher road in a hurting situation; when you let go, you feel better and move faster through the pain and experience. What have you been dealt with? What are you holding onto and refusing to let go of? Who are you holding onto, thinking that letting go may be interpreted as a weakness? You will always win when you take the higher road.

Action Exercises for Massive Success

1. Take a trip down adversity memory lane and list three major challenges you have gone through.

2. Describe how you have used these challenges or are going to use these to your advantage.

3. What pain or struggles are you currently going through? Name them.

4. List two major pains or challenges you must let go of to be free to pursue your goals with gusto.

5. Identify three main opportunities from your challenges to use to achieve massive success.

Chapter Five

Awaken the Genius Within

*"You create your life, and you can recreate it, too. In times of economic
downturn and uncertainty, it's more important than ever
to look deep inside yourself to fathom the sort of life you really want
to lead and the talents and passions that can make that possible."*
~ Ken Robinson

To be all that you were born to be you need to awaken the genius within so that you can do all the things you want to do in your lifetime. You need to recreate yourself by tapping into the creativity within you in order to achieve your dream, your purpose, your calling and mission in life. It was Einstein who said that insanity is equal to doing the same thing over and over again and expecting a different result. If you don't like your current results then change it. If you don't like the way you do things you can change that too, to start doing things a different way. Recreating yourself is about transformation and change; transformation for better results, changing your belief system to attract whatever you want, and being able to take the required actions and steps to achieve your goals. Charles Bukowski captured recreating yourself in a few beautiful words. He said, *"Invent yourself and then reinvent yourself, don't swim in the same slough. Invent yourself and then reinvent yourself and stay out of the clutches of mediocrity. Invent yourself and then reinvent yourself, change your tone and shape so often that they can never categorize you. Reinvigorate yourself and accept what is but only on the terms that you have invented and reinvented. Be self-taught and reinvent your life because you must; it is your life and its history and the present belong only to you."*

"Life isn't about finding yourself. Life is about creating yourself."
~ *George Bernard Shaw*

If you are hungry and committed to fulfilling your potential, live a great life, live a blazing trail for others to follow, and impact people with your aspirations, then you have to recreate yourself. You have a finite amount of time on this side of life and the more you waste it the more challenging it will be for you to fulfil your heart desires. You have the inner power to have it all but there are things you have to let go of to be the person you need to be, to attract the things you want in your life. It was Jim Rohn who said, "Success is what you attract by the person you become." When you become, then you can attract and not the other way round. Begin the recreation process and you will begin to see a shift in your life in alignment with where you want to go. Recreating yourself requires a shift in your thinking, the stories you keep telling yourself, the words you use, the people you associate with, the things you read, what you watch, and the actions you take on a daily basis. For things to change, you must change.

Unleash your creativity

Your creativity will take you places you never dreamt possible!

Creativity is about the effective use of your imagination to get whatever you want to build; it's about being resourceful and helping that business or person get what they want because when you do, you will get what you want. Creativity ignites your passion and vision to be more, do more, and have more. Creativity will inspire you to be a problem solver, a skill the world is in need of. You need to realize that you are a solution to someone's problem and you could just be that person a business needs to make more money, be profitable and to facilitate a conversation that will resolve a nagging business problem. You may not believe this but you are a creative human being. Your creativity is locked inside you and you have to release it to do what it was meant for. When you came in to this world, the creator endowed you with the gift of creativity. As a kid you were creative, doing a lot of things and navigating the challenges of life. As a kid you came up with various ways to get things from your parents and others. What in the world happened to that creativity? For some reason, because of your socialization process and being told by your parents, don't do this and don't do that; by your teachers, you are not cut out for this or that; by your friends, that it is a dumb idea; you have placed a lid over your creativity. It's time you release your creativity once again and change your life. There are various ways to unleash your creativity. Here are a few: release your dreams by looking at the world differently, make space for real thinking, be open-minded to see opportunities, be creative by doing things in different ways, find out what people need and want and make it available to them, look for the opportunities and possibilities around you, acquire the necessary knowledge and develop your skills, stop negative self-talk, and don't allow your false belief system, thinking patterns, mindset and preconceived ideas taint your judgment.

Years ago I read the story by Dr. Russell Conwell. Russell Conwell became very famous for his traveling lecture in which he encouraged listeners to find their "acres of diamonds" in their own backyards. Russell was born in Massachusetts in 1843, and during the Civil War served as a captain in the Union army. He studied law, but became a Baptist minister and a popular public speaker. "Acres of Diamonds" was his most famous talk which he delivered over *6,000 times*! This made him one of the great speakers of his time. At the heart of "Acres of Diamonds" was a parable Conwell heard while traveling through present-day Iraq in 1870. Here is an excerpt from the story:

"There was once a wealthy man named Ali Hafed who lived not far from the River Indus. 'He was contented because he was wealthy, and wealthy because he was contented.' One day a priest visited Ali Hafed and told him about diamonds. Ali Hafed heard all about diamonds, how much they were worth, and went to his bed that night a poor man. He had not lost anything, but he was poor because he was discontented, and discontented because he feared he was poor. Ali Hafed sold his farm, left his family, and traveled to Palestine and then to Europe searching for diamonds. He did not find them. His health and his wealth failed him. Dejected, he cast himself into the sea. One day, the man who had purchased Ali Hafed's farm found a curious sparkling stone in a stream that cut through his land. It was a diamond. Digging produced more diamonds – acres of diamonds, in fact. This, according to the parable, was the discovery of the famed Diamonds of Golconda."

The moral of the story is that oftentimes we look for answers outside of ourselves. If we are not doing well, we look for solutions from external sources when the answers lie within us or around us. We look for fortunes outside ourselves and dream of making money from elsewhere when we could be living in the heart of our acres of diamond. We need to begin looking for opportunities that are within us and closer to us. Russell Conwell also narrated other stories, including the discovery of gold in California, a farmer in Pennsylvania who sold his farm for $833 and went to work for his cousin in Canada, collecting oil. Shortly after, the man who purchased the farm found oil worth millions of dollars. Look within you, use what you already have, appreciate the lot you were given, and build something beautiful on this lot. Your acres of diamond are right beneath you. Stretch and use your imagination! If you can see it you can get it!

You are better than you think

"You're better than you think," I whispered. "I didn't realize it when I was little, didn't understand that look in your eyes, why you always looked so sad, but I get it now. Someone got inside of you and messed you all up, made up down and left right so now you think you're shit when you're not even close. So you need to listen to me when I tell you that you are better than you think. You're even better than that. To me, you're the best."
~ Eva to Deuce (Undeniable)

One of the keys to success is to believe that you have the potential and are gifted to succeed. The way you see yourself greatly affects the results and actions you take. The stories and lies you repeat to yourself every single day will impact your ability to perform in any given task or work. The mistakes you have made in the past do not define you and you are not equal to your mistakes. The business deals you have lost, the rejections you have received as a salesperson, the losses you have incurred do not diminish you. I want you to remember this for the rest of your life: *YOU ARE BETTER THAN YOU THINK!* This is a fact and not just my opinion. We achieve a small percentage of what we are capable of because of a lack of self-confidence and negative self-talk. We have allowed the results on the outside to define what we can do. One of the tragedies of life is to repeatedly tell yourself that it is impossible. Do you know that when you remove the IM from impossible you get the word possible? Any time the word impossible shows up on your radar, make a conscious effort to mentally remove the IM and think it's possible. That little shift in your thinking process will revolutionize your life. A switch in your thinking will significantly affect the direction of your life. You have come too far to conclude that you do not have it. You have come through so many experiences and life challenges to want to give up. You are better than you think. Most of the successful people we know today, Les Brown, Zig Ziglar, Brian Tracy, Jack Canfield, Jim Rohn, Denis Waitley, Tony Robbins, Oprah Winfrey and others were not successful from the start. They started from humble beginnings and worked their way up. Each of these giants of success kept their dreams alive and stood their ground, the test of time, and became the icons of success we read about today. Stop sabotaging yourself with the erroneous stories you tell yourself because if you don't stop, you will continue to get the same results as before.

I was a professional speaker in Africa before immigrating to Canada some years ago. I knew I could compete for business in the Canadian market but for some reason I did not have the confidence to do that initially. I convinced myself that I was not good enough. I was held back by fear and flawed thinking. I applied to join the Canadian Association of Professional Speakers to prove to myself that I had it and still felt that I was not good enough. I enrolled in the Fast Track Speakers program to test my ability and I did very well. I won the Rising Star competition and represented the Calgary Chapter at the National Convention. That was when it dawned on me that I had it all along! The rest is now history. The more you use your skills, the sharper you get. You are more than you think. There is always room for improvement when you condition your mind to keep developing yourself, raising the bar, keeping excellence front and center in all you do, and making continuous improvement your mantra. I am reminded of the story of when Michelangelo completed his statue of the angel. He was asked how he produced something so magnificent, and he responded, "*I saw the angel in the marble and carved until I set him free.*" You are better than you think and you have to free the genius and masterpiece within you. Starve your wrong thoughts and erroneous beliefs. Stop feeding on negativity and start feeding your possibilities. When you come to the conclusion that you are better than you think, you will begin to do amazing things that were already there right from the start.

Affirm each day "*I am very thankful and grateful that – I am smart, resourceful and brilliant; I help those who need my help; I am kind;, I invest in my growth and development; my future is great; I inspire people with my aspirations; I am changing lives; I believe in the beauty of my dreams; I live the life I have imagined; I use my talents, treasure and time wisely; I am financially free; I have multiple streams of income; I am healthy and full of vitality;, there is a major conspiracy to bless me every single day; and I have victory and success everywhere I go."*

Feel free to write your own affirmations after you have gotten acquainted with the idea. Let me warn you; when you start doing this, you will feel very silly, but don't stop. I felt the same way some years ago when I was introduced to the concept of affirmations. Affirming what you want and want to be is a spiritual law. Say those things that are not as if they were! Speaking your affirmations will open the doors to true abundance, choices, options, and doors of opportunity. Francis Colon said, *"Every moment in life, every opportunity is a choice to innovate and have an impact."*

Visualize your possibilities

"I've discovered that numerous peak performers use the skill of mental rehearsal of visualization. They mentally run through important events before they happen."
~ Charles A. Garfield

Visualization is a precursor to achieving massive success!

Napoleon Hill said, *"What the mind can conceive and believe, it can achieve."* Learning to think like a winner and visualizing what you are good at will help you move toward your dream. Make a mental movie or blueprint of what you really want in life and go after it. Try to see it, feel it, and believe that it is possible, then go to work and make it happen. When you want to soar like an eagle, you have to refuse to sit back, sigh and wish things were different. You can't just sit and complain about your lot in life and refuse to build something beautiful on the lot you were given. Be active and visualize in your mind what you want to achieve. Don't allow the challenges of life to push and hold you down. Fall if you must. Falling every now and then will happen, but keep your eyes on the goal and continue to look up for help because help is always available. Dream of the life you want, visualize it as if you are watching the movie of your life unfold and you are the main character in the movie. Visualize this in great detail, believe you can have this life, make a plan on how you are going to achieve this and move into action. A dream will remain a dream until acted upon. The words of Jim Carrey echo the point of visualization and taking action. Jim puts it this way *"I would visualize things coming to me. It would just make me feel better. Visualization works if you work hard. That's the thing. You can't just visualize and go eat a sandwich."*

John Kehoe expanded on the concept of visualization by saying, "*You are living simultaneously in two worlds, two realities: the inner reality of your thoughts, emotions and attitudes, and the outer reality of people, places, things and events. Because we fail to separate these Inner and Outer worlds, we allow ourselves to become dominated by the Outer world of appearances, and we use the Inner world solely as a 'mirror' for whatever happens to us. Our Inner world reacts constantly and because we spend all of our time simply reacting, we never experience our power. Ironically, you begin changing your reality the day, the hour, the minute you cease constantly reacting to it.*" This statement amplifies the point that when we continue to react to the external environment instead of using our higher faculties of perception, will, intuition, reason, memory, and imagination, we limit ourselves and diminish the power to achieve our dreams. You have power over your mind – not outside events. Realize this and you will find strength, said Marcus Aurelius. Lucius Annaeus Seneca pointed out, "*Without leaps of imagination, or dreaming, we lose the excitement of possibilities. Dreaming, after all, is a form of planning.*" Imagination is the way that we can test and experience our future and our dreams. Psychologists have proven that when we vividly imagine something with emotional intensity in our conscious mind, we impress it on the subconscious mind and produce the same emotional and biochemical reactions in our body as the actual experience! This observation explains why Olympic athletes use visualization in their training program. They know that when they visualize, they are getting virtually the same benefits as actually training, and by visualizing they are doing every routine perfectly! Keep out of your mind what you do not want and keep your mind on what you do want. Losers visualize the penalties of failure. Winners visualize the rewards of success! Mark Twain said, "*Twenty years from now you will be more disappointed by the things that you didn't do than by the ones you did do. So throw off the bowlines. Sail away from the safe harbour. Catch the trade winds in your sails. Explore. Dream. Discover.*"

Build your life like a scientist

> "*What lies behind us and what lies before us are tiny matters
> compared to what lies within us.*"
> ~ Ralph Emerson

A scientist is an individual who uses scientific methods to achieve a given objective. Scientists try to figure out how things happen, are very curious and like to solve problems, and they observe, measure and communicate their findings. Great scientists have vision, a passion for results, are risk takers, resilient, curious, open minded and free of bias, seek solutions, are patient and persistent, have strong observational skills, are purposeful, resourceful, good communicators, persistent, creative, critical thinkers, courageous, and objective.

In order to build your life, you must have a vision for your life. What do you want in life? Have you clearly identified these wants? Have you developed a personal vision statement for your life to guide and direct your steps? Without a vision you will continue to drift like a ship without a rudder. A personal vision statement captures what you would like to be, have and do. It defines where you want to be in the future and reflects your values, goals, and purpose. Your vision statement will answer the questions – where you want to be, your optimal desired future state, the movie of your life, i.e. a mental picture of what you want to achieve within a specific time frame, and provides direction and inspiration for the journey. Take the time to write down your personal vision statement. Building your life like a scientist requires you to have passion for results because results are the name of the dream. A great scientist is a risk taker. Risk takers know that they will win sometimes and fail sometimes. Risk takers are willing to learn from their mistakes and fail forward. Risk takers take the chance of investing in themselves with the hope of reaping the fruits in the future. Take the necessary risks in starting that business, in writing that book, in building that school, hospital or clinic, and so on. Mark Zuckerberg, founder of Google said, *"The biggest risk is not taking any risk... In a world that is changing really quickly, the only strategy that is guaranteed to fail is not taking risks."*

Winston Churchill repeated a grade during elementary school and, when he entered Harrow, was placed in the lowest division of the lowest class. Later, he twice failed the entrance exam to the Royal Military Academy at Sandhurst. He was defeated in his first effort to serve in Parliament. He became Prime Minister at the age of 62. He later wrote, *"Never give in, never give in, never, never, never, never – in nothing, great or small, large or petty – never give in except to convictions of honor and good sense. Never, Never, Never, Never give up."*

Fred Smith, the founder of Federal Express, received a "C" on his college paper detailing his idea for a reliable overnight delivery service. His professor at Yale told him, "Well, Fred, the concept is interesting and well formed, but in order to earn better than a "C" grade, your ideas also have to be feasible."

Thomas Edison's teachers said he was, "too stupid to learn anything." He was fired from his first two jobs for being "non-productive." As an inventor, Edison made 1,000 unsuccessful attempts at inventing the light bulb. When a reporter asked, "How did it feel to fail 1,000 times?" Edison replied, "I didn't fail 1,000 times. The light bulb was an invention with 1,000 steps."

Walt Disney was fired by a newspaper editor because "he lacked imagination and had no good ideas." He went bankrupt several times before he built Disneyland. In fact, the proposed park was rejected by the city of Anaheim on the grounds that it would only attract riffraff.

Albert Einstein did not speak until he was four years old and did not read until he was seven. His parents thought he was "sub-normal," and one of his teachers described him as "mentally slow, unsociable, and adrift forever in foolish dreams." He was expelled from school and was refused admittance to the Zurich Polytechnic School. He did eventually learn to speak and read. Even to do a little math!

Henry Ford failed and went broke five times before he succeeded. R. H. Macy failed seven times before his store in New York City caught on. You can see from the various stories that success does not happen overnight, and you don't have to discount yourself or talk yourself out of the great opportunities that lie ahead of you. When you don't give up and keep pursuing your goals and dreams, there is a greater chance of succeeding when you keep on keeping on. Building your life as a scientist requires you to be resourceful by looking for ways to explore various possibilities; being purposeful in all you do with the belief that you can contribute to changing your part the world; being persistent in the midst of challenges and adversity; not giving up when things are not going the way you want; being creative in using your imagination to resolve challenges and problems; and maintaining an open mind to explore different avenues and possibilities.

Action Exercises for Massive Success

1. You are a creative person. Identify four things you can do to use your creativity to achieve your goals in your area of expertise.

2. List four lies you have told and are telling yourself that are limiting what you are capable of doing.

3. Find time this evening to go to a quiet place and visualize all the things you want to be, to do, and to have, and write it down like your future story captured in the now.

4. Capture the movie of your life as you would like to see it. Include the sights and sounds so that whoever reads it will feel the emotions, see the details, and be astounded.

5. Make a list of the things you will start doing right away to begin building your life like a scientist.

Chapter Six

Thoughts are Things

"Thoughts lead on to purposes; purposes go forth in action; actions form habits; habits decide character; and character fixes our destiny."
~ Tryon Edwards

I am very fascinated with the subject of thought and thinking. I am a student of the mind and will continue as a student for a very long time. We cannot exhaust the study of the mind and the impact of our thoughts on the results we get. Your mind is a gold mine! All the things you will ever achieve in your lifetime begin from your mind. Your mind holds the key to all the possibilities and opportunities available to you. You can use your mind to create, innovate, and achieve phenomenal results beyond your wildest imagination. I believe our school system has failed millions of people for not teaching people how to think. I believe any school that has a subject on thinking and the effective use of the mind will produce more successful and high achieving people than others focusing on the normal curriculum. The more I study the mind, the more there is to discover. I encourage you to be a student of the mind. It will not only intrigue, energize, invigorate, or inspire you, but will open your mind to the possibilities that lies within you. If you can master the effective use of your mind, your results will be staggering! Do not explore the power of the mind for the sake of just understanding how it functions, but rather use it to change your life, inspire others to change, and use it to influence and impact the direction of your life. What are you using your mind for? The great discoveries and inventions of our time started in someone's mind. The changes and transformation in society began with a few thinking people. The automobiles we drive, the aeroplanes we fly in from place to place all started as an idea. What ideas do you have that you have not yet brought to life? What great pictures have you painted on the canvass of your mind that you have kept just as a fantasy? Eknath Easwaran said, *"The things we think about, brood on, dwell on, and exult over influence our life in a thousand ways. When we can actually choose the direction of our thoughts instead of just letting them run along the grooves of conditioned thinking, we become the masters of our own lives."*

You can influence your personal results by your thinking and you can also ruin your chances of success by what you think about most of the time. I have countless stories of people swimming in the back waters of poverty and living average lives by the way they think. Some believe that someone closest to them is causing them to fail. There is a belief in some quarters of the world that a lack of success or achievement in some homes and individuals are a result of evil spirits. Lazy people hide under this belief and waste their lives. Life is too short to let it slip away with excuses. It is a travesty to relinquish the leadership of your life to false beliefs, people, systems, and others when you can and should take control of your life. Hear me and hear me good; you can change the direction of your life by changing the way you think and what you think about. Many lives have been destroyed because of erroneous thinking. Have you thought about what you are thinking about lately? Do you think about what you are thinking about? Your success or failure is hidden in your thinking patterns! When you change your thinking you sure can change your results. It all starts with thought! The Bible recommends how to think and what to think about. It says, *"Summing it all up, friends, I'd say you'll do best by filling your minds and meditating on things true, noble, reputable, authentic, compelling, gracious – the best, not the worst; the beautiful, not the ugly; things to praise, not things to curse..."*

There are a number of people who allow the environment or the external to determine and influence how they think. The environment should just be your looking glass and not determine how you behave and the results you get. William James captures this well in this quote: *"Why should we think upon things that are lovely? Because thinking determines life. It is a common habit to blame life upon the environment. Environment modifies life but does not govern life. The soul is stronger than its surroundings."*

Thoughts Create Reality

Use your thoughts to create an amazing future –
You become what you think!

"Be careful of your thoughts, for your thoughts become your words.
Be careful of your words, for your words become your actions. Be careful of
your actions, for your actions become your habits. Be careful of your habits,
for your habits become your character. Be careful of your character,
for your character becomes your destiny."
~ Chinese proverb, author unknown.

Your current results can be summed up using this formula:

Thoughts ❯ Feelings ❯ Emotions ❯ Actions ❯ Results (Things)

Whatever thought you entertain and hold in your mind will create a positive or negative response or feelings. That feeling will ignite certain emotions, positive or negative. Depending on the intensity of the emotions, it will either lead to specific actions or inaction and this is what leads to the results you get. Simply put, your current results first originated in your thought life. As within, so without! Your current results are a manifestation of your inner condition which begins in your thought life. You can change your results by changing your thoughts that created the results in the first place. When you learn to appreciate and apply the thought-result connection, you will be able to change the trajectory of your life and achieve all the goals you have set for yourself. You should spend time and make an analysis of your thought life. Be honest with yourself as you analyze your thoughts. You will realize that most of your habitual thoughts are the paradigms controlling your life. You act and behave in consonance with your thinking patterns. You have been conditioned to think a certain way and since you can't be any different from your thoughts, your current state is a summation of all the thoughts you have engaged in for all these years. When your thinking changes, your results also change in tandem!

Your thinking patterns have created your current realities and results and if only you begin to watch what you allow into your mind, you will be able to influence the quality of the results you are getting. In my quest to understand why I do the things I do, act the way I do, why people behave the way they do and do the things they do, and why people will resist change and transformation even if the change is a good thing, I went on a hunt for information to understand the paradox. My search led me to a profound discovery which can be summed up in the words of James Allen, *"You are today where your thoughts have brought you; you will be tomorrow where your thoughts take you."* This statement objectifies the fact that you are responsible for your current results and will be responsible for your future results. You will continue to create your current realities through what you think about all day long. Your daily actions, behavior, attitude and routines are a result of thought. Your result as an individual is an inside job. You first create in thought, and then see the results as evidence. The pictures we paint on the canvas of our minds are creating the realities we have. Each one of us is given a LOT (portion) in life and it's our job to build something wonderful, purposeful, intriguing, amazing, life-changing, on this LOT. The question is what are you building on your LOT?

Think on purpose

> *"The whole of science is nothing more than*
> *a refinement of everyday thought."*
> ~ *Albert Einstein*

What we think we become, and true change begins with change in the mind. What change would you like to see in your job, career, family, life, health, finances, and so on?

Dr. Jack Hatkins conducted a research at the University of Tennessee. The 12 year study measured the impact of what people put into their minds. They had a control group and non-control groups listen to a five minute daily radio program, then they tested them. The results were: if there were four negative items in the five minute radio program, the listeners were 1) more depressed, 2) believed the world was a negative place to live, 3) were less likely to help others, and 4) began to believe that what they heard would actually happen to them. Five minutes of empirical research revealed so much about what we feed the mind. Five little minutes of listening to four negative things impacted them that much. Thomas Troward said, *"We cannot really think in one way and act in another."* Now imagine how your life is changing and being impacted by the things you are feeding your mind. What are you listening to, what are you reading, what are you watching, what mental diet are you on? Whatever you are feeding your mind is shaping you into the person you want to be and the person you don't want to be.

If you want to change the results, change what you are putting into your mind. As within, so without!

The quality of your results on the outside is a reflection of the quality of the thinking on the inside. The words that come out of your mouth are a reflection of your inward condition. You can never be any different from who you are on the inside. Great results begin from the inside out! Here is great advice from Benjamin Disraeli: *"Nurture your mind with great thoughts, for you will never go any higher than you think."* Start the journey of thinking on purpose, focus and think about the life you have imagined, put your desires front and center, think about your goals every single day, and write down what you want every morning. Once a week write the movie of your life, and carry a goal card to read aloud to yourself several times during the day. When you do these things it will help you think on purpose.

Your results on the outside are a reflection of the quality of the thinking!

You have the capacity to think on purpose rather than allowing negative thoughts to dominate your thinking. Andrew Young puts it succinctly, *"I have about concluded that wealth is a state of mind, and that anyone can acquire a wealthy state of mind by thinking rich thoughts."* Limited thinking produces limited results. You will not be able to resolve the current challenges of your life with the same level of thinking. Your destiny will come from your thinking. Psychologists have echoed this. The only things affecting the direction of your life are your thoughts and its implications. As you think, so you are! What you think about most of the time will create your reality. Marcus Aurelius said, *"Our life is what our thoughts make it."* Think on purpose and change your life!

Where the thoughts go, the body follows

"Do not think that what your thoughts dwell upon is of no matter.
Your thoughts are making you."
~ Bishop Steere

Whatever thoughts we allow into our minds, our inner life will show up in our outer life. To deal with poor results on the outside, we need to address wrong thinking. Our thoughts have the power to empower, energize and engage us to do amazing things, and also have the power to cause us a lot of pain. Certain thoughts can impact our health, performance, productivity, moods and our relationships. Our thoughts will impact every area of our lives. Whether you know this or not, we all have an outer life and an inner life. Our outer life is what everyone sees, while our inner life is known to only ourselves. Our inner life includes thoughts, attitudes and motives. Our lives are shaped and reshaped by the combination of these three cousins. Thinking negatively, worry, anxiety, and fearful thoughts create a mess and a dysfunction in our lives. However, when we decide to think positive, possibility, good, encouraging thoughts we move closer to doing the things we want. You have heard it said 'garbage in garbage out'. What goes in is what comes out. What we put into our minds we get more of the same from it. James Allen said, "*You are today where your thoughts have brought you, you will be tomorrow where your thoughts take you.*" Our thoughts go ahead of us and our actions follow. When our mind is fearful, our bodies follow the fear and we experience the physical effects of stress.

When we allow negative thoughts to dominate our minds, we do this to our own detriment and well-being. You always follow your thoughts. Erica Jong said, "*You take your life in your own hands, and what happens? A terrible thing: no one to blame.*" You have great power, potential and talent on the inside of you, so why not use it to create the life you want? You have the ability to do the things you have never dreamt you could do. Begin to reprogram your way of thinking so you can take concrete actions in alignment with where you want to arrive in life. I have read stories of people who used the power of the mind to achieve their goal. An example is a homeless person with no money who becomes a multimillionaire. I am referring to Bill Bartman who went from being homeless, broke, an alcoholic and paralyzed at age 17, to become the 25th richest person in the United States of America, or Mahatma Gandhi who facilitated the freedom of his people from the British Empire against all odds, or Norman Cousin who was diagnosed with a disease with little chance of surviving but went on to live many more years than his doctors predicted. These people used the power of their thoughts, reframed their experiences, took action, and succeeded. Buddha said, "*All that we are is the result of what we have thought. The mind is everything. What we think we become.*"

Build a wall around your mind

"Avoiding danger is no safer in the long run than outright exposure.
The fearful are caught as often as the bold."
~ Helen Keller

The mind is the gateway to your life. Your emotions, feelings and actions all come from what is happening in your mind. Your mind is the battleground where every war will be won or lost. Whatever you are putting in your mind is contributing to your winning or losing the battle. You want massive success, you want to achieve your goals, you want to fulfil your potential; however, there are demands from people from all walks of life needing your time and attention. Everybody wants to be in on the action of your life and be part of the movie of your life. Who should you be allowing in? What should you be allowing to participate in the movie of your life? When you become selective in what you allow into your mind, you will begin to control the direction of your life. There is so much junk and information out there asking for your time. The boss, spouse, son, daughter, friends, television, writers, significant other, books, movies, parents and so many other things asking for your time. Who and what should you give permission to be part of your life's story? Recently I decided to give myself a break from watching the evening news. I felt so much freedom and lightheadedness to pursue the things I love to do. Every single time I flip the switch on my television, what I hear most of the time is what I called negative news through and through. Within a few minutes of turning on the television I hear of this wrong and that wrong. Why don't we hear positive things about the great things happening in this great universe? There are so many wonderful people doing great things in our world and yet we focus on telling the negative stuff. This is why you should take control of your mind and allow only what you choose to allow into your mind. You can paint great pictures on the canvas of your mind. It will take your mind to build something beautiful on the lot you have been given in life. You have a choice to build a wall around your mind by simply being selective of what you allow into it. In cases when you have no choice in listening to some negative stuff, replace it immediately with the right stuff once you hear it. Every single one of us is blessed with an amazing mind; what you do with yours is totally up to you. Why not focus on what you want and keep your mind off the things you don't want? Life is not a dress rehearsal so choose what to allow into your amazing mind. Use your life to fulfil your true potential. If you could allow yourself to do all that you were born to do, it would astound you. Begin clearing your mind of all the junk and build a wall around your mind. Keep out the negative stuff and keep meditating on the good stuff. As within, so without!

You were engineered for success, you were born to do great things, and your life is a masterpiece from the creator's standpoint. Stop looking at where you are and start looking at where you want to go. Allow your mind to take you into unchartered waters and do the impossible. Let your life inspire others to do more, be more, have more, and give more for it is in giving that we are truly happy. Give your best to the people around you. Invest your life in others by using your mind for great things. Live a blazing trail so that when your life is over, you can say with all the confidence, I am thrilled for the ideas and projects that have used me.

Focus one million percent on your future

To focus is to place emphasis, attention, concentration or to single-mindedly work on something. Someone said whatever we focus on expands. We get more of what we focus on. When you want to understand why some things happen the way they do, why you are getting your current results, the first place to check for answers is your area of focus. The things we focus on become our reality. The Law of Focus states that whatever we dwell upon grows. The more we think about something, the more it becomes part of our reality. It is safe to say that our current realities are a reflection of our focus. When we think about something more often, it will eventually dominate our thinking and ultimately affect our attitude and behavior. Are you interested in getting tangible results in a specific area of your life? Focus is the answer! My observation is that we give up too easily. Discipline yourself, focus, and concentrate single-mindedly on your goals and on what you consider most valuable. The more you concentrate on what you want, the more determined and focused you will become to achieve it. The more you think about them, the faster your goals will appear and saturate the world around you. On the other hand, if you make the mistake of thinking about the things you fear, worry about various things, playing ostrich, trembling about what tomorrow will bring, these fears will soon expand and dominate your thinking and behavior instead. You will find yourself making every excuse to avoid doing the very things you need to do to achieve the very success you desire. You unconsciously sabotage yourself by thinking all the time about exactly the things you don't want to happen. Tragically enough, the more you think about the negative things, the more they grow and expand in your life as well. "*Big ideas come from forward thinking people who challenge the norm, think outside the box, and invent the world they see inside rather than submitting to the limitations of current dilemmas*" ~ Author T.D. Jakes

Action Exercises for Massive Success

1. Make a list of your dominant thoughts – what four things do you think about on a daily basis?

2. Your thoughts create your reality, so name three things you have created and are creating with your thoughts.

3. Write down three major things you want to achieve or accomplish and place these three things in a conspicuous place in your home where you can see them every single day.

4. Every single day stand in front of these three major things, and thank God for giving you these things (name each by name)." For example, if you want to earn a million dollars each year you can say something like, "God, thank you that I earn a million dollars each year" or something similar.

5. Clean your thoughts of all the negative, the junk, and those things that cause you not to do the things you want to accomplish.

Chapter Seven

Change the Way You Speak

Your results follow your words!

"Your life is a movie. You are the main character. You say your scripts and act to your lines. Of course you do your lines in each scene. There is a hidden camera and a director who you can ask for help anytime up above."
~ *Diana Rose Morcilla*

Your words have power, tremendous power at that. Anytime you speak and use words, you give those words power and your words come alive. We normally speak into existence what we believe, our desires, dreams and hopes. Your word is a living force and your words are what create your life. You are where you are because of your words and make no mistake about that. There is nothing called an idle word because each word or statement you put out there is working for you or against you. Words are living force. Words have a spiritual power and you should always speak words of possibility. When you are crystal clear in what you want in life, you can use your words to create it. Your words inspire you to take action and inspire others to do more, give more, be more, and contribute more. With your words you motivate yourself to do things you never dreamt possible and words can also create a desire in others to go to the next level. Words calm us when we are down, and words can invigorate us. Words can change the direction of your life big-time. Since words have tremendous power to change the trajectory of your life and the lives of others, be careful what you meditate on; watch the words that come from your thoughts. Remember that the actions you take flows from your words. Every single time you open your mouth to say something you are either speaking life that comes from a good heart or death that comes from an evil, distorted heart. Be careful what you say.

"Words are the most powerful thing in the universe... Words are containers. They contain faith, or fear, and they produce after their kind."
~ Charles Capps

Our words give expression to what we want, think, and feel. On one occasion, I singled out a specific team in the office, sent an email and reminded each one of them the impact they were making on people's lives. My email talked about the number of families they have helped through their efforts, the charities that are being supported, the kids that are going to school, and all the people their work was impacting. The emails I got back demonstrated that words have the power to change people's feelings and the office temperature and pulse in a very favorable way. The team was very grateful and excited about all the great things they were doing as a result of their jobs. When we help people fully understand the purpose and impact of their jobs, they are inspired and energized to do more. When the Why is clear, the How is given wings to fly! Your words are the result of your inner thoughts and attitudes. Your words are like a movie screen that reveals what you have been thinking, and your attitude and behavior. Your words can encourage, uplift, and give courage and confidence to the receiver. The right words spoken at the right time can change people's lives.

Your words give expression to what you want, think, and feel!

When you truly understand the power of words and understand that you have the responsibility of choosing how you think and what you say, your life can be totally transformed to live the life you want. John Keating said, *"No matter what anybody tells you, words and ideas can change the world."* Martin Luther King used the power of words in his *"I Have a Dream"* speech to move millions of people to action. Betty Eadie said, *"If we understood the power of our thoughts, we would guard them more closely. If we understood the awesome power of our words, we would prefer silence to almost anything negative. In our thoughts and words, we create our own weaknesses and our own strengths. Our limitations and joys begin in our hearts. We can always replace negative with positive."* Our words are like containers, they have faith or doubt. Rudyard Kipling said, *"Words are, of course, the most powerful drug used by mankind."* When my kids were young, I placed in their bedroom positive and inspirational words. When they woke up they saw those words, and before they go to bed they saw those inspiring words again. Little did I know that the words were shaping my kids' minds and lives and getting them ready to take on any challenge life threw at them during their teenage years. To this day, each of my children remembers those great quotes and words of inspiration. Words have the power to move you to do amazing things.

Your words are a clue to your problems

"Handle them carefully, for words have more power than atom bombs."
~ Pearl Strachan Hurd

To understand why you are getting your present results, listen to your own words. What are you saying to yourself and to the people around you? Your words have power. Speak words that are kind, loving, positive, uplifting, encouraging, and life-giving. Words are seeds that germinate and become reality in your life. Years ago I was facilitating a workshop and a lady participant told me she had very stupid kids. I asked her why she said that and her answer was, "My kids do so many stupid things." She continued, "I fear for their future and believe they will not amount to anything." I wanted to know more so I asked her to tell me what she habitually told her kids. She answered, "I tell them they are stupid and that if they don't stop being foolish and stupid, they will have a difficult future." Long story short, I made her realize how she was a major factor in how her kids will turn out in the future. She promised to watch her words when she returned home after the workshop. Aldous Huxley said, *"Words can be like x-rays if you use them properly – they'll go through anything. You read and you're pierced."* Choose your words carefully. I have relatives struggling and barely making it in life. When I listen to what they say, I am not surprised why they are all struggling through life. Families have been destroyed with words. Businesses have folded and closed because of words. Have you heard people say things like: I feel like dying; the way things are going I am not going to make it; I have this feeling that I am going to lose my job; the economy is so bad, I think my business is going to close very soon; and many others.

Your words will work for and against you depending on what you say most of the time. When you consciously begin to use the right words you will be amazed at the shift in the direction of your life. You have tremendous power within you so use the power of the word to release the sleeping giant within you. Use the power of words to change the results you are getting. The problems you are experiencing can be changed when you change the words you continuously use. Words can shift the direction of things in your life. I have been blessed to have traveled the world because of the work I do. I look back on my life and have seen how the words I have used over the years, and continue to use, have created and continue to create opportunities for me to live an amazing life. You can too! Hamza Yusuf said, "*Don't ever diminish the power of words. Words move hearts and hearts move limbs.*"

Speak what you want to see

"Don't let the noise of others' opinions drown out your own inner voice. And most important, have the courage to follow your heart and intuition."
~ *Steve Jobs*

You have power within you to have and achieve all that you want in life, achieve your goals, and fulfil your potential. Why not speak that into reality by the power of words and affirmations? Affirmations are statements said with emotion, confidence about a perceived truth of what you want to see in your life. Affirmations have helped thousands and millions of people turn their lives around and registered significant changes in their lives. Affirmations can be both positive and negative. You have heard stories of teachers or parents who told their kids or students very negative things, and some in their anger have said things like, "You will never achieve anything good, you are a loser." These hurtful statements do more damage than you can ever imagine. What you say stays with the people in the conscious or unconscious mind and are reinforced throughout our lives. Affirmations have the ability to program your mind into believing suggestions you have given it. The reason is the mind doesn't know the difference between what is real or fantasy.

To know your mind, listen to your words!

Speaking possibility statements or self-scripts will condition the subconscious mind to help you develop a more positive perception of yourself. Positive self-talk and affirmations can help you change harmful behaviors and accomplish your goals. An affirmation has the power to help repair the damage caused by negative scripts, those things which we repeatedly tell ourselves or which others repeatedly tell us. Write down your affirmations and read these affirmations many times during the day and before you go to sleep. It is the process of repetition that makes it firmly register in your subconscious mind. In writing your statements use the presence tense like: I earn so much each month or year, or I am healthy and following my passion of releasing champions and inspiring each one to greatness.

Here is an example of an affirmation in the present tense: *I am very happy and grateful now that: God is my source of total supply, I earn a million dollars a year, I inspire millions and am changing lives, I have multiple streams of income (MSI), I am blessed, healthy and living the life I want, I am a success, I encourage people to give of their best and be all they can be. I have great faith; there is a major conspiracy to bring good into my life. I am successful in everything I do. I am a magnet for money and abundance. I always take the higher path when faced with two choices. I am energetic and strong and I see the best in everyone and they see the same in me.*

Mark Twain said, "*Twenty years from now you will be more disappointed by the things that you didn't do than by the ones you did do, so throw off the bowlines, sail away from safe harbor, catch the trade winds in your sails. Explore. Dream. Discover.*" When you learn to speak what you want, things begin to fall into place. The words I spoke many years ago and repeated over and over again is now being actualized in my life. Begin to understand the full power of your words and all that it's doing to you. Be careful of the words you use any time you open your mouth.

Action Exercises for Massive Success

1. What have you been telling yourself? Write a brief summary on the main things you have been telling yourself.

2. For each of the things you have been telling yourself, write down 'empowers for action' or 'disempowers for action'.

3. List four major problems you have and ask yourself where these problems are coming from.

4. Check your words and see how these words or statements have contributed to these problems.

5. Write down what you want to see happen in your life and begin speaking positively about them. It is the process of repetition that will have this imprinted on your subconscious or emotional mind for massive results.

Chapter Eight

Hit Your Target!

"One of my mantras is: focus and simplicity. Simple can be harder than complex. You have to work hard to get your thinking clean to make it simple. But it's worth it in the end, because once you get there you can move mountains."
~ Steve Jobs

Focusing on one thing at a time is the key to success. Research shows that multi-tasking does not work, nor does it produce great results. Alexander Graham Bell said, *"Concentrate all your thoughts upon the work at hand. The sun's rays do not burn until brought to a focus."* There is significant power when you focus on one thing at a time. Imagine how much you would have achieved if you had concentrated all your energy on achieving your goals? We get involved in too many things and end up not doing any successfully. I know people who are doing too many things at the same time and as a result are doing poorly financially. When you focus all your time and energy into doing one thing well before you tackle another, you will have the results to show for it. You need to focus on one thing, do that one thing very well, and make that one thing the main thing. When you look at successful companies, they focus on doing one thing and doing it well before diversifying into complementary products and services. I have seen people doing a number of businesses not complementary in any form or shape and performing very poorly. Let this not be you!

When you aim at something, and I take it that your aim is to use your inner powers to achieve all that you were built for, that focused aim will help you through the tough times. Its time you aim your energy and resources in what you want the most in life. When you do you will have the results to show for it. I had a friend who got carried away with various business opportunities that showed up on his radar all at the same time. My friend thought the best thing to do was to tackle and invest in all the opportunities for fear that the opportunity would never show up again. He used all his resources and borrowed more money to invest in the various projects. He did not have the systems, people, and plans to support all these ventures. In the end he lost most of his money and was in debt for a very long time. Stop aiming at doing so many things all at the same time. When you operate on a creative plane you need not be afraid of lost opportunities. There are more than enough opportunities around you so focus and aim at the right opportunities, and use your creativity to develop and expand those opportunities. Aim at providing and bringing value to the marketplace. Aim at developing your skills so that you become more valuable to your company, your boss, and the marketplace. I constantly remind participants in my seminars that there is nothing called job security. The only security you have is the value you bring to the marketplace and the benefits that result from that.

Focus your mind like a laser!

Aim your thoughts on what you want and off the things you don't want. Aim at the bull's eye and stop wasting time on less valuable things. Apply the 80/20 rule, that 80% of your results will come from 20% of your focused area. Don't go chasing after everything, aim at the 20%. When you aim at what you want with all your energy and have developed a strategy to execute, you will have massive success. Aiming at what you want and not taking concrete action is a waste of time. You cannot hit a target that you have not set. A successful life begins with knowing precisely what you want. In my leadership and success seminars to young people, I usually ask what they want to become. I get vague answers like 'I want to be successful', 'I want to make more money', 'I want to help people', and so on. Others say they want to be a doctor, teacher, pilot and others. Clarity of the target is very important in achieving massive success. Clarity brings focused energy, time and resources to bear on what you want. It's time to focus, aim, and hit! *It is during our darkest moments that we must focus to see the light.* – Aristotle Onassis

What you focus on expands

"When one door of happiness closes, another opens,
but often we look so long at the closed door that we do not see
the one that has been opened for us."
~ Helen Keller

To focus means to put your attention on something. Focus is the path to all thinking: perception, memory, learning, reasoning, problem solving, strategy, leading, planning and decision making. Without the right focus, all aspects of your ability to think will suffer. Without focus, you will not be able to do your job effectively, let alone get the results you are aiming for. We tend to waste a lot of time without focus. Your energy will flow where your attention goes. It has always been this way and it will always be that way in the future. Where your energy goes, your attention follows! It is very important to choose your thoughts and the words you use carefully. There are people who focus on negative things and say things to support that. People say things like, 'the economy is bad', 'I have this feeling that I will lose my job', 'the newscaster talked about people dying of cancer and I am afraid I will get cancer', 'life is very tough these days', 'I am going crazy', and so forth. You will attract these negative things into your life because you are focusing on these things rather than focusing on the things you want in your life. Be careful what you focus on. Many years ago I was conducting interviews for a leadership position. I was then working for an international consulting firm and one of my responsibilities was executive recruitment. I had one gentleman who was literally begging me to give him the job. I enquired why he wanted this job so badly to which he responded, "Anytime my boss passes by my desk he always says something like 'someone is going to be fired'". This gentleman had been focusing on the statement for a while. I believe that because of his focus, he finally got fired instead of focusing on the positive and working on improving his performance.

Your energy flows where your attention goes!

I heard the story of a lady who always attracted the wrong men into her life. Each of the men she dated and got married to seemed to be the same or wrong type. They mistreated her, indulged in excessive drinking, had many partners at the same time, and were just mean to her. The words she used when looking for a different person always started with I don't want men who did this or that and her focus was on avoiding such men. However, she always attracted the same men she did not want in her life. Why? Because whatever she focused on she got more of. Why not focus your mind on what you want and off the things you do not want? Could it be the results you are getting are a result of focusing on the wrong things? The universe operates by exact laws, and when you don't do things in alignment with these laws, it comes back to get you when you least expected it.

Focusing on what is possible will enlarge your vision and bring the right people into your life to make it happen. There are people out there looking for someone with your talents, expertise and gifting. You are the solution to someone's problem and they are looking for you. Why not focus your thoughts on bringing those people into your life? I tell my audience that I believe with all my heart that there is a major conspiracy in the world to bless me big time. As a result, I wake up each morning with an expectation of increase and blessings flowing into my life from all corners of the world. I wake up with gratitude in my heart because something great is about to burst forth in my life each day. When I allow myself to have a crappy day because of something I thought about, I quickly remind myself of my identity and what I have going for me. I am having a wonderful time and my family members think that I have it made and have no problems at all.

I have learnt to speak the things I want to see in my life. I focus my thoughts on the life I want and not on the challenges around me. If you are serious about changing your life and having massive success, start with a focus on what you really want in life. This is not selfishness but rather a razor focus on what you want. You can help more people with more than enough blessings in your life. You can help others attain financial freedom and peace of mind. You can contribute significantly to making our world a better place. It all begins with what you focus on. These days I am thinking and planning to build a school in a developing world where the school will focus on helping kids, young people and adults learn the science of thinking, change, and transformation. I believe that when we change, the results, performance and productivity will change. Make a decision today to focus on what you want. Life is too short to waste it living someone else's dream. Live your dream!

Aim your energy

"The only person you are destined to become is the person you decide to be."
~ Ralph Waldo Emerson

You first become and then you attract!

like the quote by David Frost. He said, *"Don't aim for success if you want it; just do what you love and believe in, and it will come naturally."* I have attended a number of seminars in the past that amplified the pursuit of success above anything else. They talked about personal grooming, the way you speak, positioning yourself in the minds of the prospect, and all the good stuff. After years of testing the concepts I came to the conclusion that to achieve your dreams in life, you first have to know what you really want in life, what you are good at, your natural talents, then develop and sharpen your skills in that area, give value to your clients or customers, and the rest will follow. Jim Rohn captured it well when he said, *"Success is what you attract by the person you become."* In other words, you first become and then you attract. People are wasting a lot of time and energy focusing on the external rather than focusing their energy on developing themselves into becoming. Wasted energy is wasted time, resources and life as a whole. W. Clement Stone said, *"Aim for the moon. If you miss, you may hit a star."* Where are you spending your energy? Are you spending it with the wrong people who may be nice but not going anywhere? Are you wasting your resources on things that appear great but are not adding value? Are you wasting your time on how bad the economy is performing and proposed changes? What are you doing with the time you have? When you aim your energy, ensure that you are in complete harmony in thought, word and deed. *"Always aim at purifying your thoughts and everything will be well"*, says Mahatma Gandhi.

You need to aim higher and remain focused on what you want. Control the frequent vacillation between what you want and what you don't want. Paul Allen said, "You need to aim beyond what you are capable of. You must develop a complete disregard for where your abilities end. Try to do things that you're incapable of... If you think you're incapable of running a company, make that your aim... Make your vision of where you want to be a reality. Nothing is impossible." What a great way to aim your energy. Begin to dream beyond your needs to dreaming to attain your wants. When you do that you begin to stretch your imagination to achieve more.

When you align your energy with your focus on what you want, you begin to achieve results. Alignment of your beliefs, thoughts, mindset, feelings, attitudes, behavior and actions will support and set you up for achieving massively. Take a piece of paper and identify all the things you have been focusing on lately. Are they leading you to where you want to go? What can you stop, start or continue to enable your results and move the needle towards fulfilling your potential? Michelangelo said, *"The greater danger for most of us lies not in setting our aim too high and falling short; but in setting our aim too low, and achieving our mark."* To achieve massive success is to aim high, dream large, take massive action consistently until you achieve all that you have planned. While Carl von Clausewitz captures it this way, *"Pursue one great decisive aim with force and determination."*

Achieve your target

"Everything you've ever wanted is on the other side of fear."
~ George Addair

You cannot achieve a target you do not know. You will not be able to achieve massive success if you are not clear as to what you really want to achieve. Are you aware of the tools and resources you require to hit your target? How far are you from the target? Who do you need to help achieve the target? What are you currently doing that is impeding your achieving the target? Are you happy with what you have achieved so far in this target? These are great question that you should provide honest answers to in order to determine how far you are from the target. I have found that in life, unless you know where you are going, anywhere is acceptable. We have people living this way. Knowing your target and consistently hitting that target will inspire you to aim higher, raise the bar, and commit more energy and resources to the task. Achieving your target motivates you and reminds you that you have the inner resources to do more, be more and have more. Getting yourself into the habit of thinking in terms of massive results is a great way to move closer to your goals. Measuring yourself against the target and evaluating your results will help you close the gaps in achieving what you really want. There are a number of things you should do in order to hit your targets. The following are a few of the things that you should do:

Determine the importance of the target

There comes a time when you have to be crystal clear on what achieving your goals will do for you and those you love. We are not motivated and inspired to do something just for the sake of it. When the Why is clear, the How follows from there. Have you convinced yourself why you want massive success? What are the benefits in you hitting your target? Have you shared your target with your mastermind or the people important to you for support and encouragement? How different will your life be when you no longer have to worry about money? Determining your target and having a talk with yourself and those who you trust is important.

Focus on the most valuable

Make the main thing the main thing. To hit your target you must focus and commit extra energy, time, and resources to what you want. You only have a finite amount of time in a day or week. Why not focus on the most valuable things in support of the target rather than spreading yourself so thin? What are your priorities for the day or week? Have you planned your day and week in advance? The content of your dairy or plan is a reflection of what is important to you. Hitting your target requires that you focus on the most important things. You may take detours because of unexpected events, but always come back to the plan and continue with the most valuable.

Don't quit when the going gets tough

Life is full of surprises and there are more quitters than those who stay the cause. Let this not be you. Take a rest if you must, but don't rest for too long. There are times when, in the evaluation of your results, you get the feeling that you have missed the mark or target. Assess the variance and get back to work. Develop the mental toughness to proceed. I like what Dr. Robert Schullar said, *"Tough times don't last, but tough people do."* The easiest thing to do in life is to throw in the towel and quit because things are not happening the way you have planned. Challenges are to prove you worthy of your goal and the life you want. Use your challenges to be more determined to hit the target, and when you do hit the target you will be happy you never gave in to discouragement and negative self-talk.

Develop the habit of discipline

Discipline is doing the things you have planned to do even when you do not feel like doing them. There were times I arrived home from work and felt very tired. Knowing the commitment and benefits of exercising, I exercised anyway, even when I felt tired. There were times when I have heard the conversation between my left leg and the right leg on who should step out of the bed first to go and exercise. I had to arbitrate to ensure that the morning exercise program takes place. Hitting your target consistently will require discipline and continuous improvement. Develop good work habits and manage your time well. You must develop the discipline of shutting off the noises around you. Every now and then you have to keep telling that negative inner voice to shut up.

Reach out for help

Hitting your target(s) may require help from an external source. If you have a mastermind group, you can ask them for help regarding your challenges in hitting your target. I have developed the habit of prayer where I ask God for help and, sure enough, I get perspectives on what to do. I also seek advice and counsel from the people I trust. Don't shy away from asking for help. It will cut down the time for hitting your targets immensely. Always remember that asking begins the receiving process, so don't be shy. Don't listen to your feelings. Just ask, "Would you?" Asking is not a sign of weakness but a sign of strength. At least you know when to ask for help.

Let go of Excuses

We have all made excuses for not hitting our target, and many people have become very clever with excuses. When we make excuses we are failing to take full personal responsibility for our inaction and flawed plans and strategies. Be brutally honest with yourself and accept personal responsibility for not hitting your target. When you do, life will reward you greatly.

Focus on Results

"*Results tell the truth,*" someone said. What results are you getting? Your bank account and net worth reflects how well you are doing financially. Your health and how much energy you have tells you about the state of your wellness. The quality of your relationships will inform you of whether you have made great deposits in your relationship bank account. Remember, results don't lie! To hit your targets you must continuously evaluate your results. This is good practice.

Take action

> *"Everyone who has ever taken a shower has had an idea.*
> *It's the person who gets out of the shower, dries off, and*
> *does something about it that makes a difference."*
> ~ Nolan Bushnell

You may have great dreams, great strategy and plan. You may even have concrete goals for the life you want but without action, it is just a dream. Action gives fuel and wings for your dreams to fly. Taking massive action is a trait of all successful people. Most, if not all, people have the desire to achieve massive success but few get to do it. We all want the good life and each has a definition of what the good life looks like. In general we want good health, financial freedom, great relationships, to have peace of mind, and so on. Others want a life of abundance and prosperity.

Action gives wings for your dreams to fly!

To impact the world with your aspirations, run successful businesses, live an extraordinary life, meet great people who are the movers and shakers in our world and do something great, and to leave a legacy, you have to take concrete actions consistently to achieve these things. To enjoy a life of opulence and have a great life requires taking massive action to achieve your goals. Most people have goals they want to achieve but don't have the discipline to see it through. Others are fearful of taking the necessary actions needed to move the needle in the direction of their goals. You are where you are today because of the actions you have taken and you will be somewhere tomorrow because of the actions you have failed to take. Your current results are not an accident but rather all the actions you took and those you did not take. How consistent are you regarding taking massive action? You may have all the knowledge and skills in doing some-thing but without action you will not achieve much. You have heard it said that, "Knowledge is power." I disagree with that statement. What brings power is the right knowledge applied consistently for results. If you don't take action using the right knowledge, then you are not going to get the results you want. Most people have some knowledge; others have the right knowledge but don't apply that knowledge or take action on the knowledge. It is those who use the knowledge to do something, solve a problem, change something, transform an organization, or create or innovate are the ones adding value and creating value in the marketplace. Having lots of knowledge you just keep in your head is not useful to anyone; until it's applied it will provide little benefit. Do you want to accomplish great things in your lifetime? Taking action is a precondition for that to happen.

Here is your formula for massive results. ***Right thinking or thoughts + right feelings + right knowledge/skill + massive action = massive results.***

When you take massive action, you get massive results. It all depends on you. There is a correlation between your belief system and your actions. Belief drives your thoughts, which drives your feelings which drives your actions, and ultimately drives your results. If you have disempowering beliefs it will impact your behavior and also the level of action you take. You can change your beliefs to drive your behavior and actions. There is a quote in the Bible which says, "*If you can believe, all things are possible…*" When you change your belief you can change your behavior and change your results by taking action. Fear stops a lot of people from taking action. To conquer fear, we need courage. Winston Churchill wrote, "*Courage is rightly considered the foremost of virtues, for upon it, all others depend.*" Fear is, and will continue to, hold people captive from doing what they want to do. Fear has always been and will always be the greatest enemy of all humankind. When Franklin D. Roosevelt said, "*The only thing we have to fear is fear itself,*" he was, in effect, saying that the emotions of fear, rather than the reality of what we fear, is the cause of anxiety, stress, and unhappiness. Develop courage in the midst of fear and a whole new world of possibilities will open up to you. It is a natural law that if you do nothing, nothing will happen; if you take minimum action, results are going to be minimal. But if you take massive action, then you will be rewarded with massive results. Successful people who started with nothing and made million will tell you that the key to success is taking massive action even in the face of adversity.

Talk is cheap!

"The only person you are destined to become is the person you decide to be."
~ Ralph Waldo Emerson

Take your mind back to all the things you have said you will do to achieve great success. Think about the goals you have set and promised yourself you will take action on. Imagine if you kept all those promises you made to yourself and to others. What a great life you would be living right now! Talk is cheap indeed. It is very easy to say 'I will do this or that', but actually doing it is the key. Many businesses have been built in the air by just talking about them. I have a relative who kept saying, 'I will do this and that for my mother one day when I make the money.' Every year he said the same thing. I believe he meant well but never backed his promises up, then the mother passed away. One of the regrets this relative had to live with is the pain of not fulfilling his promise to his mother. I knew he was struggling with this and continues to struggle because he told me that his biggest regret was not fulfilling his promise to his mother. Talk is cheap and whoever came up with this statement is accurate and reflects the position of millions of people around the globe. Words carry a lot of weight when we use those words to fulfill all the things we want to do. When you get into the habit of saying things that you will not actualize, it will come to a point when you begin to doubt your own words and, most importantly, you begin to lose credibility with people because you did not keep your promises.

I like the words of Ernest Agyeman Yeboah who said and I paraphrase, 'Until you press the switch to turn on the light in your room, you will always have the light, but still live in darkness.' This means you can be well intentioned but until you back what you want to do with action, or until you do what you say you will do, it is wasted effort. Words become powerful and laser guided when followed up with actions. The phrase 'action speaks louder than words' are so true. Get into the habit of taking action and you will begin to trust yourself with your promises and the promises you make to others. Your credibility hinges on backing your words with action. You devalue yourself by not keeping your promises. Use your words to inspire you and others into action. Get into the habit of following through what you have promised and watch your life turn around for the better. I have come across businesses that have lost out to peers because they did not keep their promise or deliver on their promises.

I had associate consultants I worked with in the past who I don't work with anymore. The reasons were that they never kept their word on delivering reports on time for me to meet my commitment to my clients. I have had trainers who never put in the time to prepare quality presentations to deliver first class training even though they promised to do so in the first place. Keeping your word is the mark of a professional. Bringing value to the marketplace is not only about your expertise and honing down your expertise, but also delivering on your promises. It will be great to develop the reputation of doing what you said you would do. Let people begin to have the confidence in you that when you say something you deliver on all your promises. Businesses have been destroyed because of broken promises. Relationships have gone down the drain because of not following through on promises, lives have been damaged because of excuses and more excuses for not following through with promised actions. If you are really hungry to succeed and have massive success, and I believe you want to do that, just keep your promises, will you? Are you hungry for massive success? It all begins with fulfilling your promises to yourself and others in your network. Don't be known as the person who is just a talker but as someone who says something and follows through until every bit of the agreement is fulfilled. Make it a point to develop the discipline of taking action and keeping your side of the bargain. When you change, your results will change.

Action Exercise for Massive Success

1. What is your daily focus? Is it what you want or what you don't want? List what you focus on daily.

2. Where do you spend most of your energy during the day? Clearly identify where your energies go each day.

3. What targets have you set for the week and month? On a scale of 1-5, how are you performing against your targets?

4. Make a list of your daily actions and ask the question: Are these actions leading me in the direction of my goals?

5. Make a list of the things you have said you would do and did not do, ask yourself why, then take corrective action.

Chapter Nine

Your Beliefs Create the Fact

"Believe that life is worth living and your belief will help create the fact."
~ William James

Years ago when we were kids, my mother was diagnosed with what was described as a terminal illness. The doctor called my dad and gave him the sad news that his wife had a short time to live and therefore he should spend more time with her before she passed on. Dad didn't know what to do after hearing the doctor's advice. Mum was finally told what the doctor said and that was when she declared that she would not die but would live to see her children grow, have their own children, and see her grand-children as well. As kids we used to see our mum not feeling well but did not know the details of what she was suffering from, nor know the news that we only had a few months left with our mother. Talk about the power of belief! First mum heard the prognosis and knew the implications, but was not ready to leave her kids at a tender age without their mum. Mum got into a fighting mode for her life. According to mum, when she told us the story, she was ready to do whatever was humanly possible to stay alive for her children. She also had this strong belief that she would live and not die prematurely. She explored all medication that would make her well, prayed a lot for divine intervention, believing that there is a God who wants her well and for the best for her life. She meditated and visualized herself well, saw her children all grown up with their own families. My mother made it to age 82, full of vitality all the years until she passed on. We grew up, got married, had children, and visited Mum with our children for years before she passed on. There is power in what you believe and say to yourself.

I visited a lady I knew a while back at the hospital who was diagnosed with cancer. On one of my visits I asked her whether she was ready to pass on, to which she said no and that she had unfinished business. You may be wondering why on earth I asked her such a question. I did it to understand whether she was ready to fight till the bitter end, as well as to know the best way and approach to encourage her. The more she kept her mind and belief on what she wanted to complete in her life, the more she had the strength to keep living. For as long as she kept her mind on what she wanted to complete, she always remained positive and upbeat. On this particular day, I went for a visit and saw that she was not as vibrant as she had always been. When I enquired what she was thinking about, her response was that I have completed the unfinished business and now it's time to go. I was on a trip out of town when I got the sad news from her family that she had passed on. I spoke at her funeral and used the opportunity to speak about the power of belief. For as long as she maintained the belief that she had more to do, she kept going till she finally changed her position that it was time to go. Belief is a powerful force.

My last but not least story on belief is regarding a government utility corporation I did some consulting work for. This government corporation was losing money and had a lot of debt. The government was under excessive pressure to privatize the company and sell it to potential investors who would turn the corporation around. One man, the new Managing Director, believed that with a great leadership team, he would be able to turn things around and make this large government utility company perform and be profitable. He convinced the powers that be not to sell the company and he was able to turn the corporation around. With the belief that he could turn things around, he assembled a new leadership team made up of old and new managers. He worked with the team to clean up the mess, inspired the new team to focus on results, negotiated performance contracts with regional operational units, sought for help to design an exceptional customer service program to guide all operational areas, and further helped align the leadership team around performance benchmarks. Within a few short years, the corporation starting making money, was out of the red, and became a resounding success story of belief backed by sound business strategies and management practices with a highly inspired and result-focused leadership team. As a result of this resounding success, this government utility corporation started a consulting company to help other struggling government utility companies turn things around. If you believe, all things are possible!

Discard wrong beliefs

"If you don't like how things are, change it! You're not a tree."
~ Jim Rohn

Wrong beliefs affect your health, mind, achievement, progress and success. A belief anchors your understanding of the world around you; it is the state of mind in which you think something to be the case. It's an assumption and conviction that you hold to be true regarding concepts, events, people, and things. Beliefs can be empowering, inspire action, turn a desperate situation around, catapult you to the pinnacle of success, and cause you to achieve massive success. A lot of people are struggling in life because they have allowed themselves to be manipulated by a wrong belief system. A lot of the excuses and challenges I heard from participants in my seminars are as a result of crippling belief systems. People attend courses, get inspired, are exposed to what they need to change, they develop strategies and goals to change the situation, but they don't do it. Why? The answer lies in a new word I found called PRAXIS. Praxis is the integrating of belief with behavior, meaning that if your beliefs are sound and you integrate this belief into your behavior and take massive action, you create what you want.

You will never do more than the beliefs you hold. Beliefs influence action or inaction. I have met countless people who believed that something can be done when the rest of the world said it cannot be done. I have also come across people who the doctors said will never be able to walk again and yet they did. I have consulted with businesses where the shareholders felt the business had no chance of surviving but it did with a few people who believed they could fix the problem. Who are you listening to? What books are you reading? What are you watching on a daily basis? What are you telling yourself? Who is influencing your mind? Beliefs are powerful and your beliefs will create the fact!

I have a relative who I will call John for the purpose of this story. This young man is an A-student, very brilliant in his academic work, and was given bursaries for his brilliance in school. He was doing great until he started spending so much time on the internet. To his parents, John was researching academic stuff on the internet to enhance or progress his academic life. The parents started seeing a shift in behavior after a while; John wanted to be alone rather than socialize with friends and family members. The parents were concerned about the changes so they probed to see what might be happening. To their surprise, John was not searching for resources on the internet to enhance his academics but rather got hooked to a religious group that had greatly influenced and manipulated his belief system to the point that he now felt that going to school was a waste of time, the world would soon end, money would lose its value, and banks would collapse. With this belief, John went and borrowed money, got into significant debt, and is not able to pay it back. He still believed that the world would be ending soon and all his woes would be over. At the writing of this chapter, John stays at home watching YouTube and waiting for things to change, not knowing that when he changes his erroneous beliefs he will change his results and current conditions. What happened to this brilliant boy? His new beliefs are creating the fact and reality he is living with. We all need to discard our wrong beliefs. Are your beliefs enabling you to move in the direction of your dreams or are they creating conflict in your mind? Are your beliefs empowering you to be more, do more and leave a legacy of hope, inspiration, massive action, and massive results, or are your beliefs causing you to do the basic minimum? Get rid of wrong beliefs and you'll achieve massive success.

Belief creates the fact

"Be not afraid of life. Believe that life is worth living,
and your belief will help create the fact."
~ William James

The dictionary defines belief as acceptance by the mind that something is true or real, often underpinned by an emotional or spiritual sense of certainty. Your belief system will always set the tone and direction of your life. To achieve massive success you need to anchor your belief that this is possible, and your belief, cemented by your emotions, will help create the reality. As William James rightly put it, *"Believe that life is worth living and your belief will help create the fact."* To achieve massive success begins with the belief that you can. Trusting in your God-given abilities and talents to achieve whatever goal you have set for yourself is possible, but only if you believe it to be possible. As pointed out earlier, we live in a wonderful world and there are amazing things happening in our world. It's sure a great time to be alive because of the possibilities lurking around us. Never before in the history of humankind has there been so many innovations, inventions and remarkable discoveries. Keep reminding yourself that this is a remarkable time to be alive and celebrate your aliveness!

A radio station brought their sales team for a two day course at my training center several years ago. In the group were those with some sales experience and others just starting in the selling profession. When they came for the program, a few of them owned a personal vehicle while the majority did not. I challenged them to go sell big time so that by the time we met next, each would have bought a personal car fully paid for from their own funds after a year. I also made a prediction that in a year or two, those who followed the principles and concepts, and believed that they could be great sales persons would amaze themselves and write their own checks. When I met them for a refresher course after one year, the majority were driving their own vehicles. Not just any vehicle but expensive cars, for that matter. When I asked the question how it happened that most of them were now driving their personal vehicles, the answers were "We believed it when you made the prediction and we never doubted that we couldn't. We went to work, made several sales calls and sales because we believed it was possible." The two who were not able to buy their own vehicles came up with excuses why they were not able to make enough sales. When you believe that it is impossible for you to fail and you go to work to succeed, you sure will.

Let me share with you a story about my dad. My dad was a hardworking man who did very well in various businesses for some time, and lost a lot of money as well. He was very responsible and made sure that he provided for us in tandem with his financial resources. He was also a creative and good businessperson. I remember a time when the business did not do well and we were sent away from school for lack of payment of school fees. My dad started a school to take care of our needs during that period. There were very few students in the school but it served the purpose for the time being. My favorite past time in school was when we sung and went for sporting activities. Our teacher was a great musician so he taught us various songs. We were in that school for a short period and moved on to more established schools later on. I then left home to pursue a higher education, got married, had children, and visit home every year. On this particular occasion of my visit, my dad had just come from a funeral service of a friend and described in detail how he felt and reflected on his own mortality. After a couple of days, my dad made a statement that I wished he never made because it came true, just like he had said and believed. My dad talked about how, at age 70 and above, the health of people begins to give way and that he would not like to live beyond age 70. My dad's belief that at age 70 people's health began to deteriorate was not the absolute truth. My dad died at age 70 just as he had believed and spoken about. Be careful what you believe, say, and focus on. My dad's belief created the fact. Very sad indeed but that is the law of the universe. You attract to yourself what you believe and what you focus on.

Enabling beliefs

To enable is to facilitate, assist, aid, empower or make possible. Enabling belief make it possible for you to achieve massive success and achieve your goals. Enabling beliefs lead to growth, success and happiness. It facilitates possibility thinking and empowers you to take action. Enabling beliefs have caused people to amaze themselves by doing things they did not originally think possible. Enabling beliefs cause you to move forward, take risk and achieve your goals. There is power and a force that comes with enabling beliefs. Enabling beliefs include being optimistic about things rather than being pessimistic. Optimism believes that the glass is half full rather than half empty. Optimism says there will always be light at the end of the tunnel, and it's darkest before dawn. When you are optimistic you have a more cheerful disposition, which influences others to like you and support you more. Optimistic people are more resilient and will pick themselves up, dust themselves off and get on with life. Enabling beliefs are about knowing that the right attitude produces good results, the belief 'I CAN' despite all the challenges.

The flip side of enabling beliefs is limiting beliefs. These beliefs constrain us rather than release us to do the things we want to do. So many people are living impoverish lives because of these beliefs. People sell themselves short because of a certain belief system. Limiting beliefs will impact your self-image, self-concept and self-identity, and generally your perception of others and the world as a whole. Some self-limiting beliefs come with statement like 'I can't', 'it's impossible', 'it can never be', 'it's too costly', 'I am not able', 'my education is inadequate', 'this is not for me', 'nobody in my family can go that far', and so on and so forth. It's time you shake off those limiting beliefs and start doing things and taking massive action in spite of your fears, anxieties and flaws. Just go ahead and try it and you will see that you have been given the ability to achieve whatever you put your mind to, then take concrete actions to support it. You might say, "How would I know if what I want to do is going to work?" Don't worry; you will know sooner rather than later – your results will tell you. You won't know what you are capable off until you make up your mind to try, and be persistent. The word 'UNTIL' is a powerful word. Keep believing until, keep working until, keep saying the right things until, keep taking massive action until, keep providing service excellence until, and keep developing yourself until… You get the drift don't you? What results are you getting? Are you happy with your current results? If not, check your belief system and take corrective action. A few questions to help you do this are: What beliefs do I need to embrace to achieve massive success? How have my current beliefs impacted me financially, emotionally, and socially? What are some of the key things I need to do differently, and which enabling beliefs do I have to embrace and leverage to my advantage?

Action Exercise for Massive Success

1. Write down, in one sentence, your understanding of what beliefs are.

2. List all your personal beliefs, along with those passed on from parents and family, teachers, friends, media, coaches, speakers and others.

3. Identify your main beliefs driving and enabling your results, and those stalling your results.

4. Identify five beliefs you want to use to drive massive results.

5. Start the process of eliminating wrong beliefs immediately.

Chapter Ten

Goal Setting and Goal Achievement

"Setting goals is the first step in turning the invisible into visible."
~ Tony Robbins

Over 2000 years ago Aristotle described goal setting as follows, *"First, have a definite, clear, practical ideal; a goal, an objective. Second, have the necessary means to achieve your ends: wisdom, money, materials, and methods. Third, adjust all your means to that end."* The process of goal setting has been around for many years. Brian Tracy, speaking on the subject of goals, said success equals goals; all else is commentary. When you set goals it keeps you on track and causes you to focus on your goals. Each goal achieved gives you the energy, impetus and momentum to move to another goal. I have developed the habit of reviewing my goals constantly, adjusting these goals as needed, and every end of year I review all my goals and see my accomplishments for the whole year and set goals for the following year. I usually carry out this exercise the last two weeks of December and, for me, it's a very important time for reflection, asking myself the hard questions, and reviewing my results in light of my life vision and goals. When I don't accomplish some of the goals, the question I ask myself is what happened; did my priorities shift over the cause of the year? How important was the goal that I did not achieve in the grand scheme of things? Answers to these questions help me make the decision as to whether the goal should be part of my next year's goals or if I should drop it altogether.

I believe you have a system as well and if it works for you just continue with your goal setting and goal achieving system. However, if it's not working well, find a better way to evaluate your goals in tandem with what you want to accomplish. In setting your goals, remember that even though you can literally do anything, you cannot do everything. It was Denis Waitley who said, "Learn from the past, set vivid, detailed goals for the future and live in the only moment of time over which you have any control: now." This is wise advice from one of the fathers of personal development and success. Goals are very important in achieving massive success. Goals provide us with direction, bring clarity and purpose to what is important to us, and they also helps us to stay focused on what we want to do, the tasks we should be concentrating on, and helps us use our talents and potential on what matters most. If goal setting is this important, why is it that only a few people in our society set goals? The simply answer is that even though goal setting is a simple thinking exercise, only a few are willing to put in the thinking time to do it. There are those who shy away from setting goals because they believe they are too busy to make and spend the time in setting goals, some don't want to come to terms with the accountability associated with following through the goals, and for some its impatience, fear of failure and whatever else you can think of. I have a relative I taught the importance of setting goals and what it will do for them. They gave me the impression that they got it but never took the process seriously. They continue to run their business and go through life without goals. When I ask, "What is your goal for the business, family, career development and others?" I get the same answer, "Like, I want to make it and grow my business." What makes sense does not always get done and that is why massive success is a way of thinking and doing things.

I have personally combined three goal setting and goal achieving methods from three of the world's greatest on personal development and success – Zig Ziglar, Jim Rohn and Brian Tracy. These three giants of success and others have left a legacy of hope, inspiration, motivation, success, performance, advancement, and productivity for generations to come. I have decided to capture the steps in goal setting by Zig and Jim for the purpose of this chapter. After reading through the two methods, make a decision regarding the one you feel most comfortable using, put this book down, and get a pen and paper or use your computer, tablet or any other device you are currently using to complete the exercise.

Zig Ziglar said that goal setting takes a lot of time, especially when you want to do it right. This is your life and it's important you take the time to set goals. Zig also suggested that setting a goal and doing it right can take a lot of time; however, the payoff is significant. I highly recommend you set aside a few hours or adequate time to set your goals.

Step 1: State the Goal

State your main goal and make it as clear as possible. An example would be if you want to attain your ideal weight, state it clearly by stating something like "By December 30, 2017, I have achieved my ideal weight of 155 lbs." Author Brian Tracy suggests you put it in present tense as if you've already achieved it. Get to work and set your goals in the present tense.

Step 2: Set a Deadline

The second step in setting a smart goal is by setting the time you want to see your goal accomplished by. You need to have a specific timeframe in mind by which you want to accomplish your goal or goals. In the example above I said December 30, 2017. You should be able to evaluate or assess the results of your goals.

Step 3: Identify the Obstacles

Identify all the things that might stop you from realizing the goal or goals. I found this step very useful, like knowing in advance the possible challenges I might encounter and having a plan to sidestep those challenges or work around them. What are those things that may come between you and your goal? Make a list of those things and have a game plan to work on those challenges. In helping my clients through a strategic planning process, we always have to identify obstacles to success and critical success factors; once we have identified these we go to work to fix those challenges and obstacles, without which we would not be able to achieve the strategic objectives and plans.

Step 4: Identify the Individuals, Organizations, or Community You May Need for Help

Who in your network will you need in support of your goals? If you don't have anybody in your mastermind network to help, who can you tap into from the outside to help support and achieve your goals? Put a list together and you will be amazed at the resources you have available at your disposal to help move your dream forward. There is a way to get information these days more easily than ever before. Use Google or any other search engine to find out who is out there doing what you want to do or with the resources you require to support you.

Step 5: List the Benefits of Achieving the Goal

We are motivated by what we will gain or achieve when the work is done. Paint a picture of how your life will be different when you achieve your goal or goals. When you can vividly picture the gains when your goal is achieved, you have more energy, passion, and the inspiration to stay the course. Allow your imagination to run rampant and see clearly the finish line when the goal is achieved.

Step 6: List the Skills You Need to Acquire to Attain the Goal

To achieve your goals, you will require the knowledge and skills to do whatever you have set out to do. If, for example, you want to write a book and have it published, get the knowledge and skills to do that. If you want to self-publish there is tons of information on how to do this too. Identify the skills you will need to achieve your goals and make the time to acquire it. It will serve you well!

Step 7: Develop a Plan

You have survived step one through six and that is a great achievement and great news. Now is the time to put it all together using the information acquired from those steps so that you can see a detailed plan and the flow of the plan in one place. I remember years ago when I learned the needed techniques and actually developed the plan, I felt a sense of freedom and could not wait to begin implementing the plan right away. I have been setting goals for the past 20 years and it's been great. What I know is that you can accomplish your dreams and achieve massive success when you set goals and follow through with your goals. It takes time but it's all worth it. Schedule the time to develop detailed activities and an action plan in support of your goals. Try it and you will agree with me that the feeling is exhilarating. I love it!

The second goal setting system you can use is Jim Rohn's goal achievement model. Use it, work it, and help others with your accomplishments. In Jim's words, 'study, practice, teach'!

Step 1: List Five Things You Have Already Accomplished and Are Proud Of

Review what you have already accomplished to date in your life. This is about starting your goal setting on a positive note. You have achieved a number of goals in your life and this is the time to bring that to the forefront of your journey. This is great because we tend to forget what we have already accomplished and start feeling that we have not done much at all. Take a step through achievement memory lane and you will be astonished to know that you have accomplished so much already. It's all a matter of perspective. Recount your achievements on your way to massive success.

Step 2: Think About What You Want In the Next Ten Years

This is when you do real thinking regarding what you want. What matters to you? What will really make you happy? What are your purposes, calling and mission in life? What do you think you were born for? Some of these questions will help inform you on what you want in the next ten years.

Step 3: Make a List of 50 Things You Want to Accomplish

Make a list of all the things you want to accomplish. This allows you to let go of your imagination in tandem with all the things you want and helps you with long term thinking as opposed to only short term thinking. What are all the things you want to achieve? Don't be concerned about how you are going to achieve it, and don't look at where you are currently but rather where you could be. Let your imagination do the work for you. Just imagine what your life will be like when you achieve all the things you want. The key word here is what you 'want' and not what you 'need'. We are motivated by our wants rather than our needs. Write as fast as you can everything that comes to your mind and let your mind run free. Don't think of any limitations. This is not a list of what you "think you can get"; don't put any limitations on this. Think about what it is you want and imagine you could receive anything and everything you asked for. Write as fast as you can anything that comes to mind – from places you want to visit, investments, relationships, career, personal development, children, spiritual things, personal things, business things, investment properties, experiences you want to have, and vacations you want to take. A good question to ask when you go blank is, "If I could have anything I wanted, what would it be?" And keep writing until you compile the list.

Step 4: Go Through the List and Determine When You Want to Accomplish Each Item on the List

Next to each statement write a 1, 3, 5, or 10. The number "1" represents what you want to accomplish within 1 year, "3" = 3 years, "5" = 5 years and "10" = 10 years. Just as an example you could have something along the following lines:

What I want to Accomplish	
List	Priority 1-10 years
Build a condo complex	4
Build business head office	3
Write a book	1
Develop training materials	1
Vacation in France and New Zealand	2
Write the lyrics for my song	1
Set up a new business	2
Buy a vacation property	3
Etc.	

Step 5: Look at All of the Items You Marked 1, Identify the Top Four, and Create a New List of the Top 4 Things You Want in One Year's Time

For each item write down WHY you want it, what it will do for you, and what you will accomplish from it. Why did you pick this one, why is it important to you? Make sure you write at least 3-4 sentences.

When your "why" gets stronger, the "how" gets easier. When you do not have strong, powerful, clear goals the "how" becomes almost impossible. Purpose is stronger than the objective. For example, it is great to want to live in a million dollar house. However, there is more power in the "why" you want it or "what for?" than just wanting it. You must understand what you want it for. What do you feel it will bring to you? What emotions, feelings, or satisfaction will you get as a result?

Step 6: Go Through Your List and Treat Them as Goals

Count the number 1, 3, 5, and 10's you have and write down how many of each. You do not want all 1's and no 5's or 10's. Make sure you have a good balance and have enough goals to keep you excited, inspired and going. You must challenge yourself in order to grow and feel fulfilled in life.

Step 7: Think About What Type of Person You Must Become in Order to Accomplish Your List of Goals

Write down at least three to four sentences describing the person you must become in order to accomplish your list. Jim Rohn's mentor told him something that changed his whole way of thinking. He said, "You should make it your goal to become a millionaire because of what it will make of you to achieve it." The major reason you should set goals and work to attain them is what and who you become when you achieve those goals.

Take the list of your four top goals and set a date for when you will achieve them. It is VERY IMPORTANT to take immediate action, no matter how small, on each goal. Momentum is the key. Review your goals daily, see yourself already accomplishing these goals, think about how it will make you feel when you accomplish it, and get the feeling of your "why" you want them.

Act as if you can never fail.

> *"Believe and act as if it were impossible to fail."*
> *~ Charles F. Kettering*

Thousands, and even millions, of people around the world have refused to attempt a number of projects or things because of the fear of failure. Most dreams have never gotten off the ground for the fear of losing or failing. I heard it said that failure is only an event and is not final. There are people who have refused to start businesses for fear of losing their money. Others don't want to get married because of the rate of divorce around the world and what they are reading and hearing. There are people who have sold themselves short, remaining in jobs below their potential and doing jobs they hate because of fear. The statement by Charles F. Kettering, to believe and act as if it was impossible to fail, is great advice. You have the potential, the talent, the wisdom, and the resources to achieve massive success. You will encounter challenges like all the others but rest assured, it's all worth it when you attain your dreams. You are in great company though since you are not alone working toward your dreams. There are those afraid to step out and step up to do what is necessary to live their dreams. There are those making excuses that others have given away; they gave up on them years ago. Unless you try and give your dream the best shot, you will never know whether you are able to or not. You can never know how wide the rubber band will stretch unless you test it. Likewise, you can never know what you are made of, the capacity you have, the genius you have allowed to be trapped inside you unless you stretch for what lies ahead rather than focus on what you left behind.

If you knew you would not fail, would you step out and do all the things you want to do? How do you know in the first place that you will fail if you have never gone this route before? Acting as if it was impossible for you to fail is a great attitude and way of thinking. This belief and attitude will help you try things you were afraid of doing and help you smash through the barrier of fear by doing things you're afraid of. There were people who were afraid to try out something; the fear kept hold of them for a long time until they tried it and realized that it was not all that difficult.

When I was at the university, I kept hearing my friends talk about how statistics was difficult and uninteresting. The more I listened to them the more I postponed taking a class in statistics. I would not be able to graduate without taking and passing this class though. I had to first tell myself that I would not fail this course and got the courage to take it. I continuously reminded myself that it was impossible for me to fail and I did very well with a B+. I asked myself why I listened to my colleagues in the first place and why it took me so long to make the decision to take this class. Who are you allowing to speak into your life regarding what you want to do and can do? Who are you hanging around with that has contaminated your thinking to the point of inaction? If you really knew all the things you were capable of doing, you would never waste another day in procrastination. You are well equipped for greatness. The seeds of greatness were planted in you when you were born; all the resources you need to be the master-piece and champion is already in you. You have been listening to the wrong people, watching the wrong news, allowing the external environment to control your thoughts when your inner resources are screaming at you to focus inward instead of outward. Shake off your fear and anxiety and act as if you cannot fail. The worst that could happen could be missing the mark on a few things, but at least you would have known what doesn't work. Step out of your comfort zone and reach out to what lies beyond. Achieving massive success through massive action calls for you to leave your comfort zone and the land of the familiar.

Evaluate and Measure – Results are the name of the game

It is very important that you evaluate and measure your results periodically against the goals you have set. Results don't lie. If you want to know whether you are doing well financially, check your net worth and cash flow. If you want to be sure of how well you are doing in a relationship, check your emotional bank account. To know how your business is doing, review your balance sheet. There are various parameters you can use to evaluate and measure your performance in a given area. If you are a student and want to know how well you are performing in each subject area, check your grades. One of my relatives did a mock exam in order to prepare for her final high school exams. When the grades finally came in and she did not perform as required, she started blaming the teachers and school for her results. I asked her whether other students in her class got better grades to which she replied, 'Yes'. I then told her that the problem was not with the school or teachers but her. She was not happy I said that but she got the message loud and clear. Since she had another year before the final exams she was able to correct what she was doing wrong, and performed excellently in the final exams to go to the university. A lot of times people fool themselves by moving the goal post on performance and productivity and make excuses for not achieving their goals. Some are in the habit of blaming the economy, competitors, workers, change, and any other person or thing they can put the blame on. What is amusing is that none of these people accept responsibility for their role in the lack of performance. It is always the other person or the other thing. Here is a great revelation – until you take one million percent full personal responsibility for your results or lack thereof, you will not be successful in achieving massive success. Personal responsibility is about being accountable for all your results. Don't kid yourself; you are very significant in the equation of your results. You are the main character in your results. Develop the habit of evaluating and measuring your results, checking what you have done right, what you have not, and the actions you must take to close the gap. Identify the areas of performance you want to measure quantitatively and qualitatively because you cannot measure everything in quantitative terms. Establish key personal performance indicators to continuously measure your performance throughout the year. If one of your indicators is financial, how much money have you made and what was your set target? If your target is about writing a chapter of a book every weekend, a quick measure is making sure that you write that chapter. Blaming others for nonperformance is only a cop-out and who are you kidding anyway? Get into the habit of evaluating and measuring your results. You will be glad you did.

Action Exercise for Massive Success

1. Use the goal setting system above to set your goals, if you already have goals, review these goals in alignment with the model described by Zig Ziglar or Jim Rohn.

2. If you knew that you could never fail, it is impossible for you to fail, what would you like to accomplish? Write it down.

3. Begin the process of taking massive action on your goals and act as if it is impossible for you to fail.

4. Take massive action on a daily basis in tandem with your goals, and avoid the inaction excuse trap.

5. Evaluate your results on a weekly, monthly and yearly basis, and address the variance in your results.

Chapter Eleven

Tear Through the Barrier of Fear

"Everything you've ever wanted is on the other side of fear."
~ George Addair

Someone defined fear as false evidence appearing real. There is a barrier of fear that always shows its ugly head when you want to accomplish something great. This barrier terrorizes you now and again when you want to move. The barrier of fear reminds you of your past failures, brings to mind your shortfalls, and reminds you of the thousands of dollars you have lost as a result of businesses or deals you entered into. For some it's a relationship that went soar and they never want to enter into another relationship. I knew of a lady who had a difficult life because of the divorce her parents went through. This lady never wanted to have a man in her life because of what she saw the mother go through and concluded that all men are the same. No matter how hard I tried to help her understand that there are still good men in this world, she never bought it and chose to remain single. Some others have failed in a number of businesses and never want to go into any other business for themselves.

Fear has kept millions of people from following their dreams and fulfilling their potential. You are where you are because of the fears you allowed to hold you down for so long. I attended a speaker's seminar organized by Les Brown, the world renowned motivational speaker. Les is in a class of his own when it comes to motivating and inspiring people to take action.

Les talked about how for many years he kept postponing getting into the speaking business because of fear. He wasted many years of his life because he listened to his fears until he had to break through the barrier of fear. I believe Les had to get fired from a job before he fully explored the area of professional speaking. Les now speaks to millions around the world regarding breaking through the fear and doing what you are required to do. I wanted to write a book for a very long time. Several people have asked me about putting my thoughts in a book and each time I convinced myself that the time was not right. Fear also kept me from venturing out to do what I love to do, which is inspiring millions around the globe with my aspirations, until I finally had to deal with that fear. As you read this chapter, you may be held by fear, refusing to start that project because you are afraid of what might happen if it doesn't work; you have always wanted to ask your boss for a raise but are afraid to ask in case he says no. Fear is your greatest enemy and the only way to conquer your fear is to do what you are afraid of.

You have to begin to do things in spite of the fear. Fear will not disappear with inaction; you manage fear by doing the things you are afraid of. Fear is stopping you from achieving the success you want; the fear of success or failure is holding you back and time is running out. You have a finite amount of time to live your dreams here on planet earth. Each passing day that you procrastinate because of fear, you are wasting your life. Why not start anyway, because you will quickly find out if you are in the right thing or not. It takes courage to do the things you want to do and you have that courage. Your successes to-date are as a result of your courage. All that you have achieved is as a result of all the fears you have managed to work through. It will take the same discipline and belief to conquer more fears and tackle the bigger challenges in order to have the massive results you are looking for.

Whatever you require to conquer your fears is already in you. All the obstacles and challenges you went through, and may still be going through, have prepared you to deal with any form of fear. Stop telling yourself that you don't have it and stop magnifying obstacles in your mind. Do it afraid and just do it! Keep in mind that courage isn't the absence of fear, it's the ability to keep pressing on despite the presence of fear. Your solution to any fear is simply to do the thing you fear. Fear dissipates when you do the thing you fear. Start taking the necessary steps toward your goals even if it appears to be small and insignificant in nature. Actions, like pictures, are worth a thousand words. Sir Isaac Newton's principle states a *"body at rest tends to remain at rest, and a body in motion tends to remain in motion,"* Begin at once to take the first step toward your goals, take the second and then the third, and you will be on your way to doing the things you are afraid of attempting.

What are you afraid of?

"Too many of us are not living our dreams because we are living our fears."
~ Les Brown

One of the greatest challenges we all face is conquering fear and developing the discipline and habits of doing things afraid, and conquering and managing the fear. Fear has its place in our lives, especially if it inspires us toward our goals and dreams. As a professional speaker, I still experience fear every single time I have a speaking engagement. The fear causes me to prepare to deliver an exceptional presentation. I was recently talking with my wife regarding a specific talk I was about to give and the fears I had. Her response to me was that you have been doing this for many years and asked why the fear, to which I responded the fear never goes away because you never know how things will turn out. The fear only disappears when you get started and things go the way you have planned it. Winston Churchill once wrote, *"Courage is rightly considered the foremost of virtues, for upon it, all others depend."* Fear continues to remain the greatest challenge for every human being. I believe when Franklin D. Roosevelt said, *"The only thing we have to fear is fear itself,"* he was alluding to the fact that it is the emotion of fear, rather than the reality of what we fear, that is the cause of all the stress, pain, depression, lack of joy, and unhappiness in our lives.

To achieve massive success it is important that you begin to develop an unwavering self-confidence that will open all the avenues for you to live your dreams. How will your life be if you were to do all the things necessary to achieve all your goals? What will your world look like if you were to go to the places you want, live in the home of your dreams, meet the people you have always wanted to meet, run the businesses you have always dreamt of having, and doing the things you have always wanted without fear? What a wonderful life that will be! You can learn the habit of courage so that you diminish the impact of fear on your life and further deal with the various challenges that life will throw at you from time to time. Life happens to all of us and it comes to that time in your life when you need all the courage and discipline to move ahead in spite of the obstacles and challenges.

You may want to understand where our fears come from. The main source of fear originated from our childhood conditioning. The fear of failure makes us begin to think that *I can't do it, it's very difficult at the moment, I will fail like I have in the past, I will be beaten for this, and what will they think if it doesn't work out? I just have to because I have no choice.* On the basis of these fears, we start thinking of avoiding various things that may cause us to lose our investment, waste time, and be overly cautious of investing in our relationships. We want to avoid criticism from others, avoid disapproval and anything that brings discomfort. These fears can stop us in our tracks and prevent us from moving to do the things we have planned to do. Fear can paralyze you into not taking concrete or massive actions toward the goals you want to achieve. Fear can also cause indecision, procrastination, make excuses, cause hesitation and make you feel stuck.

What are you afraid of? What is stopping you from moving in the direction of your dreams? Why are you feeling stuck? Who are you associating with that seems to be amplifying your fears? What have you been told as a child that has become a stronghold in your life and causes you not to move anytime you want to take action? If your fear is the fear of failure, remember that failure is not final and failure is just an event. When you fail at something it could either be the timing may not be right, you did not do your due diligence, or you did not have the knowledge and skill to take on this assignment and do a great job at it. Most of the stories you read about successful people, you note that they have all failed many times before finally succeeding.

After graduating from my Master of Business Administration program, I was given the opportunity to speak to seasoned managers on the topic of problem solving and decision making. I did such a poor job that the evaluations I got from the participants were terrible. I felt deflated and ashamed of myself and disappointed when I read their comments. One comment said, "Never allow this young and inexperienced person to ever deliver a course to people like us." Another said, "I did not learn anything from the session and it's a waste of time, it was one deflating statement after another." I took the comments and challenge seriously and promised myself to improve and be an exceptional speaker in the near future. I had a choice to either sink or swim above the remarks and improve. I developed myself over the years and now can say with all confidence that I made it. Failure is an event and is not final. I have heard various people say that success is so hard and destroys you when you finally become a success. These people cite the cases of various people who succeeded in one area of life and finally were destroyed by their wealth. Success reveals who you truly are at your core and when you don't deal with your personal demons, they end up destroying you when you become massively successful. Prepare and develop yourself into that person who can handle massive success so that when success comes, you have a solid foundation to deal with the challenges that come with it. I have not always been a success but can now tell you that having tasted success, I prefer the life I have now than what I had in the past.

Name and isolate your fears

"Life is 10 percent what happens to me
and 90 percent how I react to it."
~ Charles Swindoll

Your ignorance of a particular situation can cause a lot of fear. We work from the information we have and when we have limited information, we feel the tension and become insecure in taking the necessary actions. Why do people fear leaving an abusive relationship where they are insecure, very unhappy, and trapped? It is the lack of information or awareness that they can start and make a great life for themselves and those around them. In one of my seminars I met a very beautiful lady who felt that her mission in life was to support her husband in achieving his dreams. I was quick to say that it is a mistake to think that way and believe there is more for her to do than live her whole life just being a support to someone else. I asked her what made her think that she was born to be a support for a guy she met and got married to. She said that she strongly believed that she was born to be a wife and a support for her husband for the rest of her life. I thought, fair enough, if that is what you believe and what you are going to do, just go ahead and live that way. The relationship fell apart; the man disappeared, left a lot of debt and, after many years, had to be located from where he was hiding. This lady's life was shattered and she is just beginning to put her life back together. For many years after the husband's disappearance she believed that one day they would come back together again. Are you in a relationship going nowhere? My suggestion is to stop looking at all the things you will lose and start focusing on all the things you will gain when you get out. When you only focus on the negative outcome from a decision, you will not be able to make the right decision to move ahead in your life.

There are millions of people around the globe who are afraid of starting their own businesses for fear of losing their capital. Some are afraid of writing that book, composing that song, or auditioning because of the fear that they might fail or not make it. I have a relative, and will call him Peter for the purposes of this story, that is doing menial jobs in the evening and is afraid of reaching out to look for other well-paying jobs. Though Peter is being treated poorly in this organization, he is afraid of leaving for fear that letting go of this job will mean he will not get another job. Ignorance of the fact that there are other jobs waiting for a person like him has kept him trapped in this job. I hope you are not like Peter. I also know another lady, let's call her Lucy, who is brilliant and can take on various jobs. Her problem is the fear of paying the price to invest in herself so she can earn more, do more and be more. Lucy has settled into a simple job making little money and working tons of hours each day. Fear has kept Lucy in her present job. I hope you are not like Lucy. Ignorance or lack of awareness has kept thousands, even millions, of people in jobs that they hate for fear of losing those jobs. When you have limited information you tend to be insecure, don't make the right decisions, and keep yourself trapped and stuck when you could be enjoying great success if you would just step out and do what you want to do. The fear of change and transformation has caused the demise of large companies we have heard of in the past, like Kodak, Compaq, EF Hutton, MCI WorldCom, Enron, Woolworth's, Pan Am, Author Anderson, TWA, The Pullmans Co., General Foods Corporation, Standard Oil, and others. Fear of personal change has caused various people to remain in the same place in life even though they don't like it. The fear of the unknown has held many people captive and reduced these people to a life of survival when, in effect, they can do more and be more with their lives.

Begin the process of naming your fear. Gather adequate information in the area you want to improve or take action, then take that action. You will become confident and start taking action when you name your fear, analyze the fear, know the source, gather information on alternative actions, and take that action. When you know the reasons for the fear, then you are poised to do what you have to do to move ahead. Get into the habit of asking yourself the question, "What am I afraid of?" As Mark Twain said, "*Courage is resistance to fear; mastery of fear is not absence of fear.*" Remember, we are all afraid of something so you are not alone. What is important is identifying the fear and doing something about it. This is what separates the successful from the unsuccessful. When you develop courage to take action in spite of fear, you will surely achieve massive success. Get into the habit of confronting your fears and your fears will diminish. Your self-esteem, self-confidence, self-image and self-concept will be on a high swing when you learn to do things even when afraid. Alternatively, when you fail to confront your fears you will be moving yourself very far from achieving your goals. Begin right now by identifying all your fears, the source of these fears, analyze what is causing them, write down how these fears are holding you down and back. Don't keep your fears – smash these fears and do things afraid.

Neutralize your fears by doing it afraid

"You gain strength, courage, and confidence by every experience in which you really stop to look fear in the face.
You must do the thing which you think you cannot do."
~ Eleanor Roosevelt

The thought of just surviving and not living the life I wanted made me very uncomfortable for years. At a deeper level I believed that life should be more than just surviving. The thought of poverty scared me because I have come across poor people and did not like such a lifestyle. I wanted more out of life so was propelled by the thought of failure to do more and be more.

I remembered the times when Dad did not have money, because during such times he wanted to be left alone most of the time. When Dad was all alone in his bedroom, you knew that he was low on cash and did not want any disturbance from any of us children. On the other hand, when Dad had lots of money, there was a lot of joy, laughter and singing because Dad played the guitar and loved to sing with us the children. The thought of a lack of money and semblance of poverty created fear in me because I did not want the life poverty or a life of not enough. Several times I felt stuck and wanted to get out of the situation but fear kept me in the same place for a long time. These fears got me thinking and on the quest to have massive success and be able to do all the things I wanted; travel to where I wanted and to do the things I wanted without thinking about money. I knew that for things to be any different in my life, I need to change, to transform my thinking, take massive action, and invest in personal development to be in a position to bring value to the marketplace.

I was hungry for information to learn about success and achievement. I invested heavily in personal development, attended seminars, bought books, audio tapes, DVDs and CD's, and got coaching from those I wanted to learn from. I invested thousands of dollars to ensure that I didn't live a life of survival and just enough, and it has all paid off. I had more money than I needed to do the things I wanted to do, and put my mum on my budget for her monthly upkeep for years until her passing. I remember one time I was called by my brother that mum was having eye problems and was going to lose her second eye if we did not do something about it. My response was to find the best eye doctor and I would pay for the operation. The operation was very successful and Mum was very happy to have her eyesight back. Another time, I thought I would surprise Mum by buying a car so that she could be driven around when she wanted to go anywhere. The car arrived before her birthday and I was informed of how Mum felt when she sat in her new car. I am telling you these stories not to impress you but to impress upon you that you can neutralize your fears, achieve massive success, achieve your goals, and be able to do much good with your money. It is a blessing to be able to do all the things I am currently doing and to have more money to give to others when the need arises. I am blessed with a great life and a great family and able to travel to where I want to go, eat what I want to eat, and do the things I want to do.

What is holding you back? What fear is stealing your joy and keeping you stuck? There is so much you can do with massive success and reaching that point in your life when you can do much good and have more than enough to live the life you want. There is nothing that can replace the smiles you bring to the faces of thousands across the nations of the world. There are people needing the solutions you bring to the marketplace. There are people ready to hear your stories of adversity to triumph. There are millions waiting for the inspiring stories of how you turned your mess into a message. Let go of that fear and do it afraid. Don't rob the world of your contributions and solutions. The future belongs to the risk takers and all those who believe in the reality of their dreams. Look for opportunities and use your talent to fulfil those needs. Don't let fear stop you! Have the courage to begin whatever you have been postponing because of fear. Start something new, step out of the comfort zone and venture into uncharted territories. Leave the land of the familiar and the shores of comfort. Success lies beyond the comfort zone. Step out in faith, and success will follow when you venture out. Dale Carnegie said, "*Inaction breeds doubt and fear.*

Action breeds confidence and courage. If you want to conquer fear, do not sit home and think about it. Go out and get busy."

Fear is mental not real

> *"Fear is only as deep as the mind allows."*
> ~ Japanese Proverb

What is your biggest fear? Is your fear real or imagined? A lot of times we let fear rule our lives and you know by now that most of the things you fear may never happen. Have you ever wished there was a pill you could take or a button you could push to eliminate fear? It appears everyone is afraid of something at some point. When we are afraid we make the following excuses: I don't have the money, I don't have what it takes, I am not ready, I don't know how, nobody in my family has come this far, what if I fail and so on. When we experience fear, our body perceives as real the present threat or danger, even if there is nothing like that. Many times we fear things that haven't even happened and often will never happen. The challenge is our brain and body can't tell the difference between real or imagined threat, so our body responds in the same way to true danger as it does to an imagined fear. Fear can take control of your mind and make it difficult for you to take any action if you allow it. Some of the symptoms of fear include: your heart beating very fast, breathing very fast, muscles feeling weak, sweating a lot, stomach churning or bowels feeling loose, finding it hard to concentrate, feeling dizzy, feeling frozen, no appetite or can't eat, hot and cold sweats, getting a dry mouth, and very tense muscles. Instead of allowing fearful thoughts, why not learn to actually listen to them and switch your internal language to be more positive? Learn to challenge your unhelpful and unhealthy thoughts and replace them with healthier thoughts. In this way you change your feelings and emotions. Replace negative thinking and start visualizing a positive future. Visualizing a fantastic future and a positive outcome, in any way and in every given situation, will destroy your fears.

Never allow your past to create fear in you. Remember, it's in the past unless you want to continue to live there. Never be so concerned about all the things you have or haven't done up until now, and never mind all the reasons why you can't, and all the people who tell you why you can't. Don't allow fear to stop you from achieving massive success; just begin and get going. Start moving decisively in the direction of the life you want.

Whatever you are afraid of is controlling your emotions, attitude, behavior, action and inaction. Whatever you are afraid of is also controlling your results. When you are ignorant and not aware of information to do something, you allow fear to dominate your thoughts. I meet people who tell me that the reason they are not doing this or that was because of a lack of money. Are you aware that all the money you require to do the things you want or to start that business is already available in the hands of someone or an institution ready and willing to give you that money provided you are aware of their existence? Ignorance is the main cause of most of your struggles.

There was a time I was so concerned with the subject of competition because that was all I knew, read and heard about. In my economics class we also learnt a lot about competition until I landed on the information about opulence, abundance and operating from a creative plane rather than a competitive plane. This information has always been available but I was ignorant and unaware of its availability. This information literally changed my life. Don't be afraid of where the money will come from to start your own business, don't be afraid of writing your book because you have little information regarding the publishing industry, and don't refuse to start something because you feel you must know everything before your new idea comes to life. Ignorance causes a destruction of your mental process that causes you to attract good into your life. Thinking in negative terms will prevent you from continuing to move onward and upward in the direction of your goal.

Having the awareness and understanding allows you to step forward and step out into personal growth and freedom. Any time you experience the emotions of doubt, fear and anxiety, just persist and it will leave. When you continue to focus on your goals and bringing value to the marketplace in spite of the fear, over a relatively short period of time your conditioning will change and you will begin the process of taking the actions you need and require to move you closer to your dreams. Playing it safe will dwarf your progress, keep you stuck, and you will live a miserable life. Sandra Gallagher, says, "*Fear and growth go hand in hand. When you courageously face the thing you fear, you automatically experience the growth you have been seeking.*" Stop fear from limiting your progress, don't step back into safety; step forward into your freedom.

Destroy and Smash the Fear Barrier

"Fears are nothing more than states of mind."
~ *Napoleon Hill (Author of* Think And Grow Rich*)*

Some fears are real while others are not. Fears that are not real are simply a mental construct. We control our fears, they don't control us. I like what Georges St-Pierre, UFC Welterweight Champion said, *"It's ok to get butterflies in your stomach; the key is to learn how to make them fly in formation."* This is well said. As a young boy we used to go out to the beach to swim. I was very terrified by the waves. My buddies were very good at riding the waves with their homemade surf boards. When we got to the beach, I played it safe by playing in the shallow waters. Several times my buddies would encourage me to go a little further into the water but each time memories of a dead person washing ashore kept me from going further. I was terrified each time we went to the beach. To make matters even worse, anytime we went to the beach and swam, we were disciplined at home by Dad who warned us never to swim at the beach. Dad was trying to protect us from being swept by the raging waves and killed in the process like others had in the past. We went anyway and were ready for the discipline whenever we were caught. I did not stop going to the beach with my siblings and friends because I loved their company. On this particular day, my friends decided to carry me into the deep end and show me that it was not all that difficult. I thought I would pass out when they threw me into the water, but I didn't. In actual fact, it felt really great to be out there in the deep end and trying my best to float and ride the waves. After trying a couple of times, I gained a level of confidence and the barrier of fear stopping me from enjoying the time with my friends started to crumble. This is why the statement 'doing things afraid' is the way to go in conquering your fears.

You need to start attacking your fears as Will Smith the actor and singer suggested. Will said, *"What developed in my early days was the attitude to start attacking the thing I was scared of."* When you start attacking what you are afraid of, the fear will dissipate. What are you afraid of? What belief system has created enormous and gigantic fears in your mind? Had I not tried going deeper into the water after my friends carried me by force to just try, I would still remain at the shallow end to this very day. There are millions of people around the nations of the world terrified to take the first step like I was when I was a very young boy. Unless you break the barrier of fear in your mind, your dream will remain just a fantasy. What you think in your head you will take action on. People break out in a sweat when confronted with the barrier of fear, just like I felt when my friends carried me into the deep water. I was very terrified, because to me, venturing into the deep end might mean death by drowning and this perception was so real I could actually see myself drowning.

James Allan, in his classic *As a Man Thinketh*, said that fear can kill a person faster than a speeding bullet. Your barrier of fear might not kill you physically but will kill your ambition of achieving massive success. Destroy in your mind all the things you are afraid of and take the necessary steps. Here are a few suggestions for smashing the barrier of fear and working through your fears: do what you are afraid of; just start what you want to do anyway in spite of the fear; be aware and acknowledge that the barrier of fear will raise its ugly head every single time you want to move forward in the direction of your goals; when fear shows its ugly head, speak to it like you would speak to a person, commanding it to go, then move on with what you want to do; get yourself excited about achieving massive success; and focus on your goals and the activities you have planned and get to work. You don't defeat fear by talking fear. Review the movie of the life you have imagined and regularly keep doing the things you love to do. Syndicated columnist Ann Landers wrote, *"If I were asked to give what I considered the single most useful bit of advice for all humanity, it would be this: Expect trouble as an inevitable part of life, and when it comes, hold your head high. Look it squarely in the eye and say, 'I will be bigger than you. You cannot defeat me.'"* This is the kind of attitude that leads to victory.

Tap into the Now

"The future is always beginning now."
~ Mark Strand

The future begins now! Every single day you are alive is an opportunity to move toward your goals and dreams. What you do now, the decisions you make today, the actions you take beginning now, can change the direction of your life. The books you start reading and the inspirational videos and movies you watch now can be a life changing event. Tap into the now! Now is the time to start the journey for massive success. There is nothing like one day. Now is the time to start that business, write that book, sing that song, go for that audition, apply for that job, send that email, forgive that person, take that action, build that bridge, and join that group. Now is the time; you have use it for doing something great. What are you doing with your now? When you learn to tap into now, it will amaze you of all the things you can accomplish. Many people have missed out on opportunities because of procrastination and the belief that 'one day' will come. I have relatives who continue to speak of 'one day' when they are supposed to be working to make that one day a success. What are you putting off because of 'one day'? Are you waiting for the future to arrive when you are supposed to create it? Don't keep telling yourself tomorrow I will do this or that. Live in the now and do what you can do today. Take the action you have been postponing now. Create that plan and work the plan now. Go out and explore the possibilities waiting for you now. Make the call to that person you have been afraid to contact now. Now is the time to take action, now is the time to change the direction of your life, now is the time to wake up from your deep sleep and realize that you have been lying to yourself for far too long. Now is the time to begin the journey to your amazing future. What you need to succeed is right inside you so get up and get going right now. Are you in a low state of mind today? Shake it off and take action. Have you lost your passion and dreams? Get it back and start now. Have you refused to get out of the house because you don't feel like going out to sell today? Let go of the pity party and reach out to your customers. Your future begins now, so do what you have to do today. The future will show up well when you participate in creating the future you want. Fear may show its head to stop you but take action anyway. The world needs your contribution, that customer needs your product, that client needs your advice or service, that person needs your solution. I have read books that have changed my life. The one who wrote it never thought that book would change the lives of millions, including me. That person heeded to the call to tap into the now and as a result, lives are being changed. Imagine all the people you will be touching when you take the action now. Your future begins now so take action now.

Action Exercise for Massive Success

1. Make a list of all the things you are terrified or afraid of doing.

2. Name and isolate these fears into different buckets. For example: financial, relationship, career, spiritual, business, tomorrow, etc.

3. For each of the fears you have identified, write down what you are going to do to smash and destroy those fears.

4. List the things you will do to build a wall around your mind since the majority of your fears are mental.

5. Do the things you fear, just do it anyway, and watch your fears dissipate.

Chapter Twelve

See the Finish Line

*What I think a lot of great marathon runners do is envision
crossing that finish line. Visualization is critical."*
~ Bill Rancic

Seeing the end from the beginning is a great way to motivate and inspire
you to achieve massive success. If I were to sit right beside you and
show you the movie of your life play by play, it would amaze you. You will
find that there are people cheering you on, those who are ready to support
your dream and goals, and all that you can leverage to your advantage. In
the movie, you are the lead character, revealed plot by plot, tackling the
various challenges, winning the various battles, celebrating the various
gains with friends, family, and associates. Have you ever played in your
mind the movie of your life as you want to see it? You are the conductor
of your own orchestra, the quality of the music, the flow, the arrangement
of the pieces are as you define it. What are you seeing 5 years, 10 years
and 15 years from now? Are you waiting for some kind of fate or you are
instrumental in the creation of the life you want? Visualizing where you
want to be or how you want to feel after you achieve massive success is very
important. It strengthens your resolve when the challenges and detours
come, it inspires you to stay the course no matter the challenges life throws
at you. Seeing the finish line in detail sets and energizes you to do more or
take massive action.

I have to continuously remind myself of how my life will be when I achieve all the goals I have set for myself. I went a step further to visualize how the lives of those my life impacts will change and that of their relations and the whole works. In my office I have visuals of most of the things I want in color. Looking at those pictures causes me to be intentional about all that I do. To me, every hour and day counts and I just don't want to waste any time doing non-essential things. I am a man on a mission to impact millions around the world before my time is done. As a practice, I frequently ask myself the question, 'Is what I am doing enabling the goals and results I want?" If the answer is no, I don't want to do it, period! I have room for some fun time as well, so it's not all about business and serious stuff. I have built into my routine some form of relaxation and recreation time. I love to have fun and I make the time for it.

Seeing the finish line is about seeing the end from the beginning. When you have a clear picture of what you want to achieve, and you can hold that picture in your mind, you are driven to achieve it. However, if you don't know what you want and how it looks, you will fumble in the dark and keep spinning for a long time. There is a science behind visualizing what you want so that you can move toward it with concrete action, energy, strength and renewed determination. Visualization to improve performance and achievement of goals is used by successful people from all walks of life.

Years ago I met a gentleman who was just starting a church and he shared with me the type of building he wanted to put up for his church, in detail. He shared how people would be pouring in from all over the city, the number of doors he envisaged on the church building to take care of the numbers coming in, where the church offices would be located, the type of people he wanted at the door to usher in the visitors, the internal décor of the church, the details of the church compound, and other details. When this friend was telling me all these stuff, he did not have a piece of property to build this church, he did not own a church building, and he had very few people who met at a school building. As I write this chapter, this friend now has a large church building with the details he had described and more. He first saw it and then built it. Here is a statement you should remember for the rest of your life – "If you can see it in your head, you can hold it in your hand." In the same way, you first need to see the finish line of the life you want and then begin the process of building and achieving it. There is a former NBA great, Jerry West who is known for hitting shots at the buzzer and acquired the nickname "Mr. Clutch". When asked what accounted for his ability to make the big shots, West explained that he had rehearsed making those same shots countless times in his mind. Other sports legends like Michael Jordan, Larry Bird, Tiger Woods and pitcher Roy Halladay also used the process of seeing what they wanted before they did it. See your finish line in great detail.

Why does seeing the finish line or the end from the beginning work? According to research using brain imagery, visualizing what you want works because neurons in our brains, the cells that transmit information, interprets imagery as equivalent to a real-life action. When we see and visualize in our minds what we want with emotion, the brain generates an impulse that tells our neurons to execute what we want to do. This creates a new neural pathway, or clusters of cells, in our brain that work together to create memories or learned behaviors to prime our body to take action consistent with what we imagined.

Picture the finish line with emotion

When you picture your future with emotion, it drives you to do amazing things. Years ago, in my quest for financial freedom, I spoke to my friend George who was farming across a beautiful lake. He got me interested in buying a lot at the same place. The day came for me to tour the entire property so I could make a decision to buy or not to buy. A few people were engaged to create a path through this forest-looking plot for me to see the property end-to-end. A few minutes through the trees, one of the guides asked, "Did you people see that huge snake sleeping comfortably in the tree up there?" The mention of a snake created so much fear in me because we were told as kids how dangerous snakes could be. I immediately thought, *I am in the wrong place and perhaps I should forget buying the property.* I was assured that there is a way to deal with snakes in the area and that I should not be intimidated at all. We continued with the process until we got to the end of the property and, voila, we were right in front of this beautiful lake. My heart started racing with all the possibilities and what I could use the property for. I no longer thought about snakes but what I could create on the property. I finalized the negotiations and bought the 12 acre property. I went home that night and started dreaming of what was possible. I thought of a training center, a camping site, an orchard, a vegetable farm, a personal recreational home to spend weekends with friends and family after work in the city and after traveling back from my seminars, speaking engagements, and consulting assignments.

I did my plan and started work on the property. In a matter of two years I had the house built, a training hall to take a maximum of 100 people at a time for training, a boat to ferry people to and from the training center across the lake, small houses for tourists to rent when they visited the property, over a thousand seedless orange trees, a large poultry farm of 7,000 birds, and other things. I tell this story to impress upon you that picturing the finish line with emotion works. I saw people coming to my training center for training, the sight and sounds of birds when I visited the place, enjoying the quiet waters of the lake as I crossed with my boat, and all the good stuff. I enjoyed developing the property, spent weekends with friends and family over years before I sold the property to immigrate to North America. I wish I could put into words the emotions and feelings I got when I was dreaming all these things and when it finally got built. You can do the same too by doing what I did; picturing the life you want, the type of success you have imagined. Whatever your mind can conceive and believe, you can achieve. I achieved what I envisioned and you can too.

Imagine your future perfect

*"Imagine for a moment your own version of a perfect future.
See yourself in that future with everything you could wish for
at this very moment fulfilled. Now take the memory
of that future and bring it here into the present. Let it influence
how you will behave from this moment on."*
~ *Deepak Chopra*

Brian Tracy likes to say, imagine your ideal future, visualize your life perfect in every respect. You can attain this future when you work on you, let go the excess baggage and take massive actions to achieve massive success. Thomas Edison said, "*If we did all the things we are capable of doing, we would literally astonish ourselves.*" This profound statement by Edison is so true. The biggest obstacle to achieving massive success is self-imposed limitations or "self-limiting beliefs". We all have them but some people have so many of these self-limiting beliefs that they are unable to take concrete actions to do what they want to do. Others are completely paralyzed by these beliefs. There are people on the continent of Africa and elsewhere, and perhaps every nation of the world, who believe that there is a person or spirit that is stopping them from realizing and pursuing their dreams. So instead of taking action, they are resigned to the excuse that their lack of success is somebody's fault. These self-limiting beliefs have stripped millions of people on this continent from fulfilling their potential and they are barely getting by. Your future can be perfect and the best way to ensure that future is perfect is to create it. A self-limiting belief can be an idea that you are limited in some way by someone, or in terms of time, talent, intelligence, money, ability, or opportunity. There is a way to be totally free from these negative constraints. One way of doing this is to change your thinking about who you are and what your possibilities are. You have tremendous opportunities available to you when you see and seize them. Knowing that what you need to have massive exponential success is already deposited in you and believing this fact will begin to shift your way of thinking. Pierre Teilhard de Chardin challenged all people with the following words, "*It is our duty as men and women to proceed as though the limits to our abilities do not exist.*" There are no limits to what you can accomplish except the limits you have placed upon yourself. Learn to integrate your empowering and enabling beliefs with your behavior and then and only then will you begin the journey to massive success. Put another way, align you with you! You are your beliefs and you are your behavior. This is why you can never be different from your beliefs.

A faulty belief system will trigger wrong behavior patterns. Bob Proctor explains it so beautifully, "*Only those individuals whose beliefs are sound... are in harmony with the laws of the universe... and have been integrated with their behavior, will emerge as real winners in the New Economy.*" By imagining your future perfect and using your inner powers and help from above, you have the potential of changing your life in amazing ways. Take, for instance, the belief that you are God's masterpiece, you have greatness in you, you have tremendous potential, you have no limitations whatsoever, and your future is perfect. You then integrate this belief with your daily routine of taking action, massive action, based on this belief. You shock yourself positively with all that you can achieve in your lifetime. You may think that your beliefs are already integrated with your behavior; however, this is far from the truth. There are times you believe one thing and do another thing. For instance, you know that you are not supposed to run the red light and doing so could result in an accident, but every now and then you run the red light anyway. Another example is the belief and knowledge that you should not spend more than you earn, yet millions are in debt as a result of continuing to spend what they do not have.

There is a gap between knowing and doing, and belief and behavior. Why not begin to analyze your beliefs and replace the erroneous beliefs with the right ones, then integrate these beliefs with your behavior and watch your results shift in the direction of massive success. Albert E. N. Gray said, "*The common denominator of success is in forming the habit of doing the things that failures don't like to do.*" Develop the habit of imagining your future perfect with all the things you want to do, the places you want to visit, the businesses you want to create, the investments you want to undertake, the houses you want to build, the contributions you want to make, the people you want to meet, the life you have imagined, and the actions you need to take to make it all come together. Imagine your life perfect without limitations. How would you like to live? Do you have that picture well developed in your mind? If you were financially independent, what kind of home would you live in? What kind of car would you want to drive? What kind of life would you like to provide for your family? What sort of activities would you like to engage in throughout the week, month, and year? I have no reservations whatsoever that you can achieve massive success. You have the DNA for that and you can achieve financial freedom so that you don't have to worry about money again. I know this because your future is perfect – and I mean that sincerely.

Action Exercises for Massive Success

1. Paint a picture of your finish line and describe in detail how your life will be when you accomplish your goals and achieve all your dreams.

2. Begin the process of visualizing your future perfect with everything falling into place according to your plans.

3. Start celebrating the small and the large wins in light of key success milestones.

4. Throw a party for yourself for completing this book and completing all the exercises. Just spoil yourself, okay!

5. Let me know how you are doing by contacting me on **info@georgeayee.com**

Summary

Every living human being wants to achieve something great, wants increase in some form or shape. Some want to be financially free while others want to leave a legacy, leave a blazing trail for others to follow. Some want to be remembered as inspiring millions for greatness and changing lives. Whatever you dream, you can achieve it and achieve it massively. The time for short-changing yourself is over. The time to remain thinking small for fear of failing is in your past. You are a great candidate for massive success. You hold in your hands the keys to improving people's lives, resolving business challenges, and inspiring and encouraging others to achieve their goals. You have in your hands the code to massive success. You can master the art of massive success. Why wait any longer when you can start now and show the world that you showed up and made the best of the life you have been given? You were not born to just exit and disappear without leaving your mark, without making your contribution. You were born for more, to be more and have more. Contentment has been taken out of context by many and represented to mean just acceptance of what life gives you, to just be happy with what you've got. Why live such a lie when you can stretch to your maximum potential and help others achieve what they want? You were created for a life of increase. Don't accept anything less.

Expand your vision, embrace your challenges, and use adversity as a springboard to achieving massive success. Silence the voices that are telling you it's not your time or you do not have what it takes. Let go of the people who remind you that success is not for you, and doubt all the statements and suggestions cocooning you into a mold of inaction and stagnation. Break out and break forth. Use your stumbling blocks as stepping stones to move you right into your destiny. Don't get tired or weary in doing good for yourself and to others. At the right time it will come back, paying you big time. When you refresh others, you will also be refreshed. This is a spiritual principle! What keeps you awake at night? What is that burning desire causing you to want to take massive action? Whatever it is, go for it and continue to take massive action UNTIL.

Never forget the word UNTIL. I believe people give up too soon. When you persist long enough and keep working your goals, before you know it, you will be achieving the success you want. Never fall for get rich quick schemes; you have been endowed with a gold mind, and have the knowledge, wisdom and power to have it all. Should you be going for anything less? Absolutely not! Use your imagination to create and achieve all that you want. You have more in you than you will ever exhaust in your lifetime. Operate from a creative plane as opposed to a competitive plane. There is more than enough to go around and there is more abundance for you to tap into. Don't sell yourself short by the suggestions you feed your mind.

Fortify your mind against the opposition and the challenges of life. When you are rejected, say 'Next'! Ask for help from above, for you have that help available. Ask for help from those who have achieved what you are looking for. Get into a mastermind group that is hungry to make a difference; leverage their skills and develop a great desire for massive success. A group of likeminded people can achieve significant results. Detoxify your relationships and only keep those who are going in the direction of your dreams. Life is too short and every day holds a piece of your future. Discount wrong beliefs and use your uniqueness to create something beautiful on the canvas of your mind. Go build your dream and enjoy the trip while building it. Remember to make somebody great on your way to massive success and greatness. I hope to meet you in person at the right time. I look to the miracle process of life to make our paths cross sooner, rather than later. I wish you significant success all the days of your life.

Dr. George Ayee

Dr. George Ayee is a consultant, professional speaker, coach and trainer. He helps his clients to unleash the full power of each organization and its employees for maximum results. George works with organizations and people to unlock the power of change and transformation for optimal results.

George's philosophy is that successful change and transformation is a precondition for optimal organizational results. Organizations and people who learn to anticipate, embrace, engage, exploit, and navigate change and transformation successfully are the leaders of their respective industries and careers. In alignment with his philosophy, George spends his time facilitating change and transformation programs, coaching leaders and people to work through change and transformation successfully.

George's passionate, inspirational, and high energy call-for-action liberates and engages his audience for action, change and transformation. His electrifying seminars on leading change, personal change, resilience in change, organizational transformation, and personal achievement, motivates his clients and audience to immediately take required actions to achieve their vision, strategic objectives and goals.

George will help you go through change and the transformation process faster and successfully.

With a doctorate in business administration, an MBA in international business administration, a BS in Finance/Accounting and decades of experience, George works with world-class companies, oil and gas companies, banks, insurance companies, non-profit organizations, government institutions, and people who want to succeed, follow their passion, exploit their potential, make more money and achieve organizational objectives.

You can contact George at:
www.georgeayee.com
georgeayee@shaw.ca

www.ingramcontent.com/pod-product-compliance
Lightning Source LLC
Chambersburg PA
CBHW061958040426
42447CB00010B/1806